TO:

_____

FROM:

_____

DATE:

_____

Be of good courage,
and He shall strengthen your heart,
all you who hope in the Lord.

—

Psalm 31:24 NKJV

The quoted ideas expressed in this book (but not Scripture verses) are not, in all cases, exact quotations, as some have been edited for clarity and brevity. In all cases, the author has attempted to maintain the speaker's original intent. In some cases, quoted material for this book was obtained from secondary sources, primarily print media. While every effort was made to ensure the accuracy of these sources, the accuracy cannot be guaranteed. For additions, deletions, corrections, or clarifications in future editions of this text, please write Freeman-Smith.

Scripture quotations are taken from:

The Holy Bible, King James Version (KJV)

The Holy Bible, New International Version (NIV) Copyright © 1973, 1978, 1984, by International Bible Society. Used by permission of Zondervan Publishing House. All rights reserved.

The Holy Bible, New King James Version (NKJV) Copyright © 1982 by Thomas Nelson, Inc. Used by permission.

Holy Bible, New Living Translation, (NLT) copyright © 1996. Used by permission of Tyndale House Publishers, Inc., Wheaton, Illinois 60189. All rights reserved.

The Message (MSG)- This edition issued by contractual arrangement with NavPress, a division of The Navigators, U.S.A. Originally published by NavPress in English as THE MESSAGE: The Bible in Contemporary Language copyright 2002-2003 by Eugene Peterson. All rights reserved.

New Century Version®. (NCV) Copyright © 1987, 1988, 1991 by Word Publishing, a division of Thomas Nelson, Inc. All rights reserved. Used by permission.

The New American Standard Bible®, (NASB) Copyright © 1960, 1962, 1963, 1968, 1971, 1972, 1973, 1975, 1977, 1995 by The Lockman Foundation. Used by permission.

The Holman Christian Standard Bible™ (HCSB) Copyright © 1999, 2000, 2001 by Holman Bible Publishers. Used by permission.

Cover Design by Kim Russell / Wahoo Designs
Page Layout by Bart Dawson

ISBN 978-1-60587-457-9

Printed in the United States of America

1 2 3 4 5—CHG—17 16 15 14 13

100 VERSES & PRAYERS OF HOPE

INTRODUCTION

There are some Bible verses that are so important, so crucial to the Christian faith, that
every believer should consider them carefully
and review them often. This text examines 100 of the
most familiar verses from God's Holy Word. These
verses, which you've probably heard many times
before, are short enough and memorable enough to
provide hope and courage for your daily journey. So
do yourself and your loved ones a favor: study each
verse and do your best to place it permanently in your
mind and in your heart. When you do, you'll discover
that having God's Word in your heart is even better
than having a Bible on your bookshelf.

For God so loved the world, that he gave his only begotten Son, that whosoever believeth in him should not perish, but have everlasting life.

John 3:16 KJV

THE GIFT OF ETERNAL LIFE

We begin with John 3:16, a verse that you've undoubtedly known since childhood. After all, this verse is, quite possibly, the most widely recognized sentence in the entire Bible. But even if you memorized this verse many years ago, you still need to make sure it's a verse that you can recite by heart now.

John 3:16 makes this promise: If you believe in Jesus, you will live forever with Him in heaven. It's an amazing promise, and it's the cornerstone of the Christian faith.

Eternal life is not an event that begins when you die. Eternal life begins when you invite Jesus into your heart right here on earth. So it's important to remember that God's plans for you are not limited to the ups and downs of everyday life. If you've allowed Jesus to reign over your heart, you've already begun your eternal journey.

As mere mortals, our vision for the future, like our lives here on earth, is limited. God's vision is not burdened by such limitations: His plans extend throughout all eternity.

Let us praise the Creator for His priceless gift, and let us share the Good News with all who cross our paths. We return our Father's love by accepting His grace and by sharing His message and His love. When we do, we are blessed here on earth and throughout all eternity.

And this is the will of Him who sent Me, that everyone who sees the Son and believes in Him may have everlasting life; and I will raise him up at the last day.

John 6:40 NKJV

MORE GREAT IDEAS ABOUT ETERNAL LIFE

If you are a believer, your judgment will not determine your eternal destiny. Christ's finished work on Calvary was applied to you the moment you accepted Christ as Savior.

Beth Moore

Teach us to set our hopes on heaven, to hold firmly to the promise of eternal life, so that we can withstand the struggles and storms of this world.

Max Lucado

Your choice to either receive or reject the Lord Jesus Christ will determine where you spend eternity.

Anne Graham Lotz

A PRAYER FOR TODAY

Lord, I am only here on this earth for a brief while. But, You have offered me the priceless gift of eternal life through Your Son Jesus. I accept Your gift, Lord, with thanksgiving and praise. Let me share the good news of my salvation with those who need Your healing touch. Amen

*Let us hold on to the confession of our hope without wavering,
for He who promised is faithful.*

Hebrews 10:23 HCSB

HE OFFERS HOPE

Despite God's promises, despite Christ's love, and despite our countless blessings, we frail human beings can still lose hope from time to time. When we do, we need the encouragement of Christian friends, the life-changing power of prayer, and the healing truth of God's Holy Word.

If you find yourself falling into the spiritual traps of worry and discouragement, seek the healing touch of Jesus and the encouraging words of fellow Christians. And remember the words of our Savior: "These things I have spoken unto you, that in me ye might have peace. In the world ye shall have tribulation: but be of good cheer; I have overcome the world" (John 16:33 KJV). This world can be a place of trials and tribulations, but as believers, we are secure. God has promised us peace, joy, and eternal life. And, of course, God keeps His promises today, tomorrow, and forever.

MORE GREAT IDEAS ABOUT HOPE

God's Word never said we were not to grieve our losses. It says we are not to grieve as those who have no hope (1 Thessalonians 4:13). Big Difference.

Beth Moore

Hope is faith holding out its hand in the dark.

Barbara Johnson

Troubles we bear trustfully can bring us a fresh vision of God and a new outlook on life, an outlook of peace and hope.

Billy Graham

I discovered that sorrow was not to be feared but rather endured with hope and expectancy that God would use it to visit and bless my life.

Jill Briscoe

A PRAYER FOR TODAY

Dear Lord, let my hopes begin and end with You. When I am discouraged, let me turn to You. When I am weak, let me find strength in You. You are my Father, and I will place my faith, my trust, and my hopes in You, this day and forever. Amen

In the beginning God created the heavens and the earth. The earth was without form, and void; and darkness was on the face of the deep. And the Spirit of God was hovering over the face of the waters. Then God said, "Let there be light"; and there was light.

Genesis 1:1-3 NKJV

CELEBRATING GOD'S CREATION

I n the beginning, God created everything: the things we see and the things we don't. And each morning, the sun rises upon a glorious world that is a physical manifestation of God's infinite power and His infinite love. And yet, because of the incessant demands of everyday life, we're sometimes too busy to notice.

We live in a society filled with more distractions than we can possibly count and more obligations than we can possibly meet. Is it any wonder, then, that we often overlook God's handiwork as we rush from place to place, giving scarcely a single thought to the beauty that surrounds us?

Today, take time to really observe the world around you. Take time to offer a prayer of thanks for the sky above and the beauty that lies beneath it. And take time to ponder the miracle of God's creation. The time you spend celebrating God's wonderful world is always time well spent.

MORE GREAT IDEAS ABOUT GOD'S CREATION

Man was created by God to know and love Him in a permanent, personal relationship.

Anne Graham Lotz

No philosophical theory which I have yet come across is a radical improvement on the words of Genesis, that "in the beginning God made Heaven and Earth."

C. S. Lewis

God expresses His love through creation.

Charles Stanley

A PRAYER FOR TODAY

Dear Lord, You have created a universe that is glorious to behold yet impossible to comprehend. I praise You for Your creation, Father, and for the sense of awe and wonder that You have placed in my heart. This is the day that You have made; let me use it according to Your will and in the service of Your Son. Amen

The Lord is my shepherd; I shall not want. He makes me to lie down in green pastures; He leads me beside the still waters. He restores my soul.

Psalm 23:1-3 NKJV

GOD'S PROTECTION

David, the author of the 23rd Psalm, realized that God was his shield, his protector, and his salvation. And if we're wise, we realize it, too. After all, God has promised to protect us, and He intends to keep His promise.

In a world filled with dangers and temptations, God is the ultimate armor. In a world filled with misleading messages, God's Word is the ultimate truth. In a world filled with more frustrations than we can count, God's Son offers the ultimate peace.

Will you accept God's peace and wear God's armor against the dangers of our world? Hopefully so—because when you do, you can live courageously, knowing that you possess the supreme protection: God's unfailing love for you.

The world offers no safety nets, but God does. He sent His only begotten Son to offer you the priceless gift of eternal life. And now you are challenged to return

God's love by obeying His commandments and honoring His Son.

Sometimes, in the crush of everyday life, God may seem far away, but He is not. God is everywhere you have ever been and everywhere you will ever go. He is with you night and day; He knows your thoughts and your prayers. And, when you earnestly seek His protection, you will find it because He is here—always—waiting patiently for you to reach out to Him. And the next move, of course, is yours.

I know whom I have believed and am persuaded that He is able to guard what has been entrusted to me until that day.

—

2 Timothy 1:12 HCSB

MORE GREAT IDEAS ABOUT GOD'S PROTECTION

The Lord God of heaven and earth, the Almighty Creator of all things, He who holds the universe in His hand as though it were a very little thing, He is your Shepherd, and He has charged Himself with the care and keeping of you, as a shepherd is charged with the care and keeping of his sheep.

Hannah Whitall Smith

Prayer is our pathway not only to divine protection, but also to a personal, intimate relationship with God.

Shirley Dobson

The Will of God will never take you where the Grace of God will not protect you.

Anonymous

A PRAYER FOR TODAY

Lord, You are my Shepherd. You care for me; You comfort me; You watch over me; and You have saved me. I will praise You, Father, for Your glorious works, for Your protection, for Your love, and for Your Son. Amen

Praise the Lord! Oh, give thanks to the Lord, for He is good!
For His mercy endures forever.

Psalm 106:1 NKJV

PRAISE HIM

Because we have been saved by God's only Son, we must never lose hope in the priceless gifts of eternal love and eternal life. And, because we are so richly blessed, we must approach our Heavenly Father with reverence and thanksgiving.

Sometimes, in our rush "to get things done," we simply don't stop long enough to pause and thank our Creator for the countless blessings He has bestowed upon us. But when we slow down and express our gratitude to the One who made us, we enrich our own lives and the lives of those around us.

Thanksgiving should become a habit, a regular part of our daily routines. God has blessed us beyond measure, and we owe Him everything, including our eternal praise. Let us praise Him today, tomorrow, and throughout eternity.

MORE GREAT IDEAS ABOUT PRAISE

Be not afraid of saying too much in the praises of God; all the danger is of saying too little.

Matthew Henry

Two wings are necessary to lift our souls toward God: prayer and praise. Prayer asks. Praise accepts the answer.

Mrs. Charles E. Cowman

Most of the verses written about praise in God's Word were voiced by people faced with crushing heartaches, injustice, treachery, slander, and scores of other difficult situations.

Joni Eareckson Tada

The time for universal praise is sure to come some day. Let us begin to do our part now.

Hannah Whitall Smith

A PRAYER FOR TODAY

Dear Lord, today and every day I will praise You. I come to You with hope in my heart and words of thanksgiving on my lips. Let me follow in Christ's footsteps, and let my thoughts, my prayers, my words, and my deeds honor You now and forever. Amen

Then the One seated on the throne said, "Look! I am making everything new."

Revelation 21:5 HCSB

New Beginnings

I f we sincerely want to change ourselves for the better, we must start on the inside and work our way out from there. Lasting change doesn't occur "out there"; it occurs "in here." It occurs, not in the shifting sands of our own particular circumstances, but in the quiet depths of our own hearts.

Life is constantly changing. Our circumstances change; our opportunities change; our responsibilities changes; and our relationships changes. When we reach the inevitable crossroads of life, we may feel the need to jumpstart our lives . . . or the need to start over from scratch.

Are you in search of a new beginning or, for that matter, a new you? If so, don't expect changing circumstances to miraculously transform you into the person you want to become. Transformation starts with God, and it starts in the silent center of a humble human heart—like yours.

MORE GREAT IDEAS ABOUT NEW BEGINNINGS

Like a spring of pure water, God's peace in our hearts brings cleansing and refreshment to our minds and bodies.

Billy Graham

God is not running an antique shop! He is making all things new!

Vance Havner

The amazing thing about Jesus is that He doesn't just patch up our lives, He gives us a brand new sheet, a clean slate to start over, all new.

Gloria Gaither

No matter how badly we have failed, we can always get up and begin again. Our God is the God of new beginnings.

Warren Wiersbe

A PRAYER FOR TODAY

Dear Lord, You have the power to make all things new. Renew my strength, Father, and renew my hope for the future. Today and every day, Lord, let me draw comfort and courage from Your promises and from Your unending love. Amen

Your heart must not be troubled. Believe in God; believe also in Me.

John 14:1 HCSB

SOLVING PROBLEMS

Here's a riddle: What is it that is too unimportant to pray about yet too big for God to handle? The answer, of course, is: "nothing." Yet sometimes, when the challenges of the day seem overwhelming, we may spend more time worrying about our troubles than praying about them. And, we may spend more time fretting about our problems than solving them. A far better strategy is to pray as if everything depended entirely upon God and to work as if everything depended entirely upon us.

What we see as problems God sees as opportunities. And if we are to trust Him completely, we must acknowledge that even when our own vision is dreadfully impaired, His vision is perfect. Today and every day, let us trust God by courageously confronting the things that we see as problems and He sees as possibilities.

MORE GREAT IDEAS ABOUT PROBLEMS

Just remember, every flower that ever bloomed had to go through a whole lot of dirt to get there!

Barbara Johnson

The happiest people in the world are not those who have no problems, but the people who have learned to live with those things that are less than perfect.

James Dobson

You've got problems; I've got problems; all God's children have got problems. The question is how are you going to deal with them?

John Maxwell

A PRAYER FOR TODAY

Dear Heavenly Father, You are my strength and my protector. When I am troubled, You comfort me. When I am discouraged, You lift me up. When I am afraid, You deliver me. Let me turn to You, Lord, when I am weak. In times of adversity, let me trust Your plan and Your will for my life. Your love is infinite, as is Your wisdom. Whatever my circumstances, Dear Lord, let me always give the praise, and the thanks, and the glory to You. Amen

Rejoice always, pray without ceasing, in everything give thanks; for this is the will of God in Christ Jesus for you.

1 Thessalonians 5:16-18 NKJV

BE THANKFUL

For most of us, life is busy and complicated. We have countless responsibilities, some of which begin before sunrise and many of which end long after sunset. Amid the rush and crush of the daily grind, it is easy to lose sight of God and His blessings. But, when we forget to slow down and say "Thank You" to our Maker, we rob ourselves of His presence, His peace, and His joy.

Our task, as believing Christians, is to praise God many times each day. Then, with gratitude in our hearts, we can face our daily duties with the perspective and power that only He can provide.

MORE GREAT IDEAS ABOUT GRATITUDE

Contentment comes when we develop an attitude of gratitude for the important things we do have in our lives that we tend to take for granted if we have our eyes staring longingly at our neighbor's stuff.

Dave Ramsey

We become happy, spiritually prosperous people not because we receive what we want, but because we appreciate what we have.

Penelope Stokes

If you won't fill your heart with gratitude, the devil will fill it with something else.

Marie T. Freeman

It is only with gratitude that life becomes rich.

Dietrich Bonhoeffer

A PRAYER FOR TODAY

Lord, let my attitude be one of gratitude. You have given me much; when I think of Your grace and goodness, I am humbled and thankful. Today, let me express my thanksgiving, Father, not just through my words but also through my deeds . . . and may all the glory be Yours. Amen

You are being renewed in the spirit of your minds; you put on the new man, the one created according to God's likeness in righteousness and purity of the truth.

Ephesians 4:23-24 HCSB

RENEWAL

When we genuinely lift our hearts and prayers to God, He renews our strength. Are you almost too weary to lift your head? Then bow it. Offer your concerns and your fears to your Father in Heaven. He is always at your side, offering His love and His strength.

Are you troubled or anxious? Take your anxieties to God in prayer. Are you weak or worried? Delve deeply into God's Holy Word and sense His presence in the quiet moments of the early morning. Are you spiritually exhausted? Call upon fellow believers to support you, and call upon Christ to renew your spirit and your life. Your Savior will never let you down. To the contrary, He will always lift you up if you ask Him to. So what, dear friend, are you waiting for?

MORE GREAT IDEAS ABOUT RENEWAL

For centuries now, Christians have poured out their hearts to the Lord and found treasured moments of refuge.

Bill Hybels

Walking with God leads to receiving his intimate counsel, and counseling leads to deep restoration.

John Eldredge

Father, for this day, renew within me the gift of the Holy Spirit.

Andrew Murray

The same voice that brought Lazarus out of the tomb raised us to newness of life.

C. H. Spurgeon

A PRAYER FOR TODAY

Heavenly Father, sometimes I am troubled, and sometimes I grow weary. When I am weak, Lord, give me strength. When I am discouraged, renew me. When I am fearful, let me feel Your healing touch. Let me always trust in Your promises, Lord, and let me draw strength from those promises and from Your unending love. Amen

Let not your heart be troubled: ye believe in God, believe also in me. In my Father's house are many mansions: if it were not so, I would have told you. I go to prepare a place for you. And if I go and prepare a place for you, I will come again, and receive you unto myself; that where I am, there ye may be also.

John 14:1-3 KJV

THIS WORLD IS NOT YOUR HOME

Sometimes life's inevitable troubles and heart-breaks are easier to tolerate when we remind ourselves that heaven is our true home. An old hymn contains the words, "This world is not my home; I'm just passing through." Thank goodness!

For believers, death is not an ending; it is a beginning. For believers, the grave is not a final resting-place; it is a place of transition. Death can never claim those who have accepted Christ as their personal Savior. Christ has promised that He has gone to prepare a glorious home in heaven—a timeless, blessed gift to His children—and Jesus always keeps His promises.

If you've committed your life to Christ, your time here on earth is merely a preparation for a far different life to come: your eternal life with Jesus and a host of fellow believers.

So, while this world can be a place of temporary hardship and temporary suffering, you can be comforted in the knowledge that God offers you a permanent home that is free from all suffering and pain. Please take God at His word. When you do, you we can withstand any problem, knowing that your troubles are temporary, but that heaven is not.

Our citizenship is in heaven,
from which we also eagerly wait for
a Savior, the Lord Jesus Christ.

—

Philippians 3:20 HCSB

MORE GREAT IDEAS ABOUT HEAVEN

Ultimate healing and the glorification of the body are certainly among the blessings of Calvary for the believing Christian. Immediate healing is not guaranteed.

Warren Wiersbe

The key to healthy eating is moderation and managing what you eat every day.

John Maxwell

Our primary motivation should not be for more energy or to avoid a heart attack but to please God with our bodies.

Carole Lewis

God wants you to give Him your body. Some people do foolish things with their bodies. God wants your body as a holy sacrifice.

Warren Wiersbe

A PRAYER FOR TODAY

Dear Lord, I thank You for the gift of eternal life that is mine through Your Son Jesus. I will keep the promise of heaven in my heart today and every day. Amen

Come to me, all you who are weary and burdened, and I will give you rest. Take my yoke upon you and learn from me, for I am gentle and humble in heart, and you will find rest for your souls. For my yoke is easy and my burden is light.

Matthew 11:28-30 NIV

ENOUGH REST?

Even the most inspired Christians can, from time to time, find themselves running on empty. The demands of daily life can drain us of our strength and rob us of the joy that is rightfully ours in Christ. When we find ourselves tired, discouraged, or worse, there is a source from which we can draw the power needed to recharge our spiritual batteries. That source is God.

God intends that His children lead joyous lives filled with abundance and peace. But sometimes, abundance and peace seem very far away. It is then that we must turn to God for renewal, and when we do, He will restore us.

God expects us to work hard, but He also intends for us to rest. When we fail to take the rest that we need, we do a disservice to ourselves and to our families.

Is your spiritual battery running low? Is your energy on the wane? Are your emotions frayed? If so, it's time to turn your thoughts and your prayers to God. And when you're finished, it's time to rest.

MORE GREAT IDEAS ABOUT REST

Jesus taught us by example to get out of the rat race and recharge our batteries.

Barbara Johnson

Satan does some of his worst work on exhausted Christians when nerves are frayed and their minds are faint.

Vance Havner

Life is strenuous. See that your clock does not run down.

Mrs. Charles E. Cowman

One reason so much American Christianity is a mile wide and an inch deep is that Christians are simply tired. Sometimes you need to kick back and rest for Jesus' sake.

Dennis Swanberg

A PRAYER FOR TODAY

Dear Lord, when I'm tired, give me the wisdom to do the smart thing: give me the wisdom to put my head on my pillow and rest! Amen

Whatever you do, do it enthusiastically, as something done for the Lord and not for men.

Colossians 3:23 HCSB

ENTHUSIASM NOW

D o you see each day as a glorious opportunity to serve God and to do His will? Are you enthused about life, or do you struggle through each day giving scarcely a thought to God's blessings? Are you constantly praising God for His gifts, and are you sharing His Good News with the world? And are you excited about the possibilities for service that God has placed before you, whether at home, at work, at church, or at school? You should be.

You are the recipient of Christ's sacrificial love. Accept it enthusiastically and share it fervently. Jesus deserves your enthusiasm; the world deserves it; and you deserve the experience of sharing it.

MORE GREAT IDEAS ABOUT ENTHUSIASM

Wherever you are, be all there. Live to the hilt every situation you believe to be the will of God.

Jim Elliot

Don't take hold of a thing unless you want that thing to take hold of you.

E. Stanley Jones

Enthusiasm, like the flu, is contagious—we get it from one another.

Barbara Johnson

One of the great needs in the church today is for every Christian to become enthusiastic about his faith in Jesus Christ.

Billy Graham

A PRAYER FOR TODAY

Dear Lord, the Christian life is a glorious adventure—let me share my excitement with others. Let me be an enthusiastic believer, Father, and let me share my enthusiasm today and every day. Amen

Ask, and it will be given to you; seek, and you will find; knock, and it will be opened to you. For everyone who asks receives, and he who seeks finds, and to him who knocks it will be opened.

Matthew 7:7-8 NKJV

ASK HIM FOR THE THINGS YOU NEED

How often do you ask God for His help and His wisdom? Occasionally? Intermittently? Whenever you experience a crisis? Hopefully not. Hopefully, you've acquired the habit of asking for God's assistance early and often. And hopefully, you have learned to seek His guidance in every aspect of your life.

In Matthew 7, God promises that He will guide you if you let Him. Your job is to let Him. But sometimes, you will be tempted to do otherwise. Sometimes, you'll be tempted to go along with the crowd; other times, you'll be tempted to do things your way, not God's way. When you feel those temptations, resist them.

God has promised that when you ask for His help, He will not withhold it. So ask. Ask Him to meet the needs of your day. Ask Him to lead you, to protect you, and to correct you. And trust the answers He gives.

God stands at the door and waits. When you knock, He opens. When you ask, He answers. Your task, of course, is to seek His guidance prayerfully, confidently, and often.

MORE GREAT IDEAS ABOUT ASKING GOD

When will we realize that we're not troubling God with our questions and concerns? His heart is open to hear us—his touch nearer than our next thought—as if no one in the world existed but us. Our very personal God wants to hear from us personally.

Gigi Graham Tchividjian

All we have to do is to acknowledge our need, move from self-sufficiency to dependence, and ask God to become our hiding place.

Bill Hybels

By asking in Jesus' name, we're making a request not only in His authority, but also for His interests and His benefit.

Shirley Dobson

MORE FROM GOD'S WORD

If you remain in Me and My words remain in you, ask whatever you want and it will be done for you.

John 15:7 HCSB

What father among you, if his son asks for a fish, will, instead of a fish, give him a snake? Or if he asks for an egg, will give him a scorpion? If you then, who are evil, know how to give good gifts to your children, how much more will the heavenly Father give the Holy Spirit to those who ask Him?

Luke 11:11-13 HCSB

So I say to you, keep asking, and it will be given to you. Keep searching, and you will find. Keep knocking, and the door will be opened to you.

Luke 11:9 HCSB

You do not have because you do not ask.

James 4:2 HCSB

A PRAYER FOR TODAY

Lord, when I have questions or fears, I will turn to You. When I am weak, I will seek Your strength. When I am discouraged, Father, I will be mindful of Your love and Your grace. I will ask You for the things I need, Father, and I will trust Your answers, today and forever. Amen

You shall have no other gods before Me.

Exodus 20:3 NKJV

PUTTING GOD FIRST

Is God your top priority? Have you given His Son your heart, your soul, your talents, and your time? Or are you in the habit of giving God little more than a few hours on Sunday morning? The answers to these questions will determine how you prioritize your days and your life.

As you contemplate your own relationship with God, remember this: all of mankind is engaged in the practice of worship. Some people choose to worship God and, as a result, reap the joy that He intends for His children. Others distance themselves from God by worshiping such things as earthly possessions or personal gratification . . . and when they do so, they suffer.

In the book of Exodus, God warns that we should place no gods before Him. Yet all too often, we place our Lord in second, third, or fourth place as we worship the gods of pride, greed, power, or lust.

When we place our desires for material possessions above our love for God—or when we yield to temptations of the flesh—we find ourselves engaged in a struggle that is similar to the one Jesus faced when He was tempted by Satan. In the wilderness, Satan offered Jesus earthly power and unimaginable riches, but Jesus turned Satan away and chose instead to worship God. We must do likewise by putting God first and worshiping only Him.

Does God rule your heart? Make certain that the honest answer to this question is a resounding yes. In the life of every righteous believer, God comes first. That's precisely the place that He deserves in your heart, too.

Love the Lord your God with all your heart, with all your soul, and with all your strength.

—

Deuteronomy 6:5 HCSB

MORE GREAT IDEAS ABOUT PUTTING GOD FIRST

It is impossible to please God doing things motivated by and produced by the flesh.

Bill Bright

You must never sacrifice your relationship with God for the sake of a relationship with another person.

Charles Stanley

Make God's will the focus of your life day by day. If you seek to please Him and Him alone, you'll find yourself satisfied with life.

Kay Arthur

You must never sacrifice your relationship with God for the sake of a relationship with another person.

Charles Stanley

A PRAYER FOR TODAY

Dear Lord, keep me mindful of the need to place You first in every aspect of my life. You have blessed me beyond measure, Father, and I will praise You with my thoughts, my prayers, my testimony, and my service, this day and every day. Amen

I am come that they might have life, and that they might have it more abundantly.

John 10:10 KJV

ACCEPTING GOD'S ABUNDANCE

The 10th chapter of John tells us that Christ came to earth so that our lives might be filled with abundance. But what, exactly, did Jesus mean when He promised "life . . . more abundantly"? Was He referring to material possessions or financial wealth? Hardly. Jesus offers a different kind of abundance: a spiritual richness that extends beyond the temporal boundaries of this world.

Is material abundance part of God's plan for our lives? Perhaps. But in every circumstance of life, during times of wealth or times of want, God will provide us what we need if we trust Him (Matthew 6). May we, as believers, claim the riches of Christ Jesus every day that we live, and may we share His blessings with all who cross our path.

MORE GREAT IDEAS ABOUT ABUNDANCE

God's riches are beyond anything we could ask or even dare to imagine! If my life gets gooey and stale, I have no excuse.

Barbara Johnson

God loves you and wants you to experience peace and life—abundant and eternal.

Billy Graham

It would be wrong to have a "poverty complex," for to think ourselves paupers is to deny either the King's riches or to deny our being His children.

Catherine Marshall

Yes, we were created for His holy pleasure, but we will ultimately—if not immediately—find much pleasure in His pleasure.

Beth Moore

A PRAYER FOR TODAY

Dear Lord, thank You for the abundant life that is mine through Christ. Give me courage to claim the spiritual riches that You have promised, and lead me according to Your plan for my life, today and always. Amen

This is the day which the LORD hath made; we will rejoice and be glad in it.

Psalm 118:24 KJV

CELEBRATE THE GIFT OF LIFE

Today is a non-renewable resource—once it's gone, it's gone forever. Our responsibility, as thoughtful believers, is to use this day in the service of God's will and in the service of His people. When we do so, we enrich our own lives and the lives of those whom we love.

God has richly blessed us, and He wants you to rejoice in His gifts. That's why this day—and each day that follows—should be a time of prayer and celebration as we consider the Good News of God's free gift: salvation through Jesus Christ.

Oswald Chambers correctly observed, "Joy is the great note all throughout the Bible." E. Stanley Jones echoed that thought when he wrote "Christ and joy go together." But, even the most dedicated Christians can, on occasion, forget to celebrate each day for what it is: a priceless gift from God.

What do you expect from the day ahead? Are you expecting God to do wonderful things, or are you living beneath a cloud of apprehension and doubt? The familiar words of Psalm 118:24 remind us that every day is a cause for celebration. Our duty, as believers, is to rejoice in God's marvelous creation.

MORE GREAT IDEAS ABOUT JOYFUL LIVING

When the dream of our heart is one that God has planted there, a strange happiness flows into us. At that moment, all of the spiritual resources of the universe are released to help us. Our praying is then at one with the will of God and becomes a channel for the Creator's purposes for us and our world.

Catherine Marshall

If you can forgive the person you were, accept the person you are, and believe in the person you will become, you are headed for joy. So celebrate your life.

Barbara Johnson

Today is mine. Tomorrow is none of my business. If I peer anxiously into the fog of the future, I will strain my spiritual eyes so that I will not see clearly what is required of me now.

Elisabeth Elliot

MORE FROM GOD'S WORD

Working together with Him, we also appeal to you: "Don't receive God's grace in vain." For He says: In an acceptable time, I heard you, and in the day of salvation, I helped you. Look, now is the acceptable time; look, now is the day of salvation.

2 Corinthians 6:1-2 HCSB

Therefore, get your minds ready for action, being self-disciplined, and set your hope completely on the grace to be brought to you at the revelation of Jesus Christ.

1 Peter 1:13 HCSB

So teach us to number our days, that we may gain a heart of wisdom.

Psalm 90:12 NKJV

A PRAYER FOR TODAY

Lord, You have given me another day of life; let me celebrate this day, and let me use it according to Your plan. I praise You, Father, for my life and for the friends and family members who make it rich. Enable me to live each moment to the fullest as I give thanks for Your creation, for Your love, and for Your Son. Amen

For by grace you are saved through faith, and this is not from yourselves; it is God's gift—not from works, so that no one can boast.

Ephesians 2:8-9 HCSB

THE GIFT OF GRACE

In the second chapter of Ephesians, God promises that we will be saved by faith, not by works. It's no wonder, then, that someone once said that GRACE stands for God's Redemption At Christ's Expense. It's true—God sent His Son so that we might be redeemed from our sins. In doing so, our Heavenly Father demonstrated His infinite mercy and His infinite love. We have received countless gifts from God, but none can compare with the gift of salvation. God's grace is the ultimate gift, and we owe Him the ultimate in thanksgiving.

The gift of eternal life is the priceless possession of everyone who accepts God's Son as Lord and Savior. We return our Savior's love by welcoming Him into our hearts and sharing His message and His love. When we do so, we are blessed today and forever.

MORE GREAT IDEAS ABOUT GRACE

In the depths of our sin, Christ died for us. He did not wait for persons to get as close as possible through obedience to the law and righteous living.

Beth Moore

No one is beyond his grace. No situation, anywhere on earth, is too hard for God.

Jim Cymbala

The Christian life is motivated, not by a list of do's and don'ts, but by the gracious outpouring of God's love and blessing.

Anne Graham Lotz

God shields us from most of the things we fear, but when He chooses not to shield us, He unfailingly allots grace in the measure needed.

Elisabeth Elliot

A PRAYER FOR TODAY

Dear Lord, You have offered Your grace freely through Christ Jesus. I praise You for that priceless gift. Let me share the good news of Your Son with a world that desperately needs His peace, His abundance, His love, and His salvation. Amen

But grow in the grace and knowledge of our Lord and Savior Jesus Christ. To Him be the glory both now and forever.

2 Peter 3:18 NKJV

SPIRITUAL GROWTH

The words of 2 Peter 3:18 make it clear: spiritual growth is a journey, not a destination. When it comes to your faith, God doesn't intend for you to stand still; He wants you to keep moving and growing. In fact, God's plan for you includes a lifetime of prayer, praise, and spiritual growth.

Many of life's most important lessons are painful to learn. During times of heartbreak and hardship, we must be courageous and we must be patient, knowing that in His own time, God will heal us if we invite Him into our hearts.

Spiritual growth need not take place only in times of adversity. We must seek to grow in our knowledge and love of the Lord every day that we live. In those quiet moments when we open our hearts to God, the One who made us keeps remaking us. He gives us direction, perspective, wisdom, and courage. The appropriate moment to accept those spiritual gifts is the present one.

Are you as mature as you're ever going to be? Hopefully not! When it comes to your faith, God doesn't intend for you to become "fully grown," at least not in this lifetime. In fact, God still has important lessons that He intends to teach you. So ask yourself this: what lesson is God trying to teach me today? And then go about the business of learning it.

Now may the God of hope fill you with all joy and peace in believing, so that you may overflow with hope by the power of the Holy Spirit.

—

Romans 15:13 HCSB

MORE GREAT IDEAS ABOUT SPIRITUAL GROWTH

We look at our burdens and heavy loads, and we shrink from them. But, if we lift them and bind them about our hearts, they become wings, and on them we can rise and soar toward God.

Mrs. Charles E. Cowman

If all struggles and sufferings were eliminated, the spirit would no more reach maturity than would the child.

Elisabeth Elliot

Grow, dear friends, but grow, I beseech you, in God's way, which is the only true way.

Hannah Whitall Smith

We set our eyes on the finish line, forgetting the past, and straining toward the mark of spiritual maturity and fruitfulness.

Vonette Bright

A PRAYER FOR TODAY

Dear Lord, Thank You for the opportunity to walk with Your Son. And, thank You for the opportunity to grow closer to You each day. I thank You for the person I am . . . and for the person I can become. Amen

Guard your heart above all else, for it is the source of life.

Proverbs 4:23 HCSB

GUARD YOUR HEART

You are near and dear to God. He loves you more than you can imagine, and He wants the very best for you. And one more thing: God wants you to guard your heart.

Every day, you are faced with choices . . . more choices than you can count. You can do the right thing, or not. You can be prudent, or not. You can be kind, and generous, and obedient to God. Or not.

Today, the world will offer you countless opportunities to let down your guard and, by doing so, make needless mistakes that may injure you or your loved ones. So be watchful and obedient. Guard your heart by giving it to your Heavenly Father; it is safe with Him.

MORE GREAT IDEAS ABOUT GUARDING YOUR HEART

Our actions are seen by people, but our motives are monitored by God.

Franklin Graham

The more wisdom enters our hearts, the more we will be able to trust our hearts in difficult situations.

John Eldredge

We can't stop the Adversary from whispering in our ears, but we can refuse to listen, and we can definitely refuse to respond.

Liz Curtis Higgs

To lose heart is to lose everything.

John Eldredge

A PRAYER FOR TODAY

Dear Lord, I will guard my heart against the evils, the temptations, and the distractions of this world. I will focus, instead, upon Your love, Your blessings, and Your Son. Amen

Then He said to them all, "If anyone desires to come after Me, let him deny himself, and take up his cross daily, and follow Me. For whoever desires to save his life will lose it, but whoever loses his life for My sake will save it."

Luke 9:23-24 NKJV

FOLLOW HIM

Jesus walks with you. Are you walking with Him? Hopefully, you will choose to walk with Him today and every day of your life.

Jesus loved you so much that He endured unspeakable humiliation and suffering for you. How will you respond to Christ's sacrifice? Will you follow the instructions of Luke 9:23 by taking up His cross and following Him? Or will you choose another path? When you place your hopes squarely at the foot of the cross, when you place Jesus squarely at the center of your life, you will be blessed. If you seek to be a worthy disciple of Jesus, you must acknowledge that He never comes "next." He is always first.

Do you hope to fulfill God's purpose for your life? Do you seek a life of abundance and peace? Do you intend to be Christian, not just in name, but in deed? Then follow Christ. Follow Him by picking up His cross today and every day that you live. When you do, you will quickly discover that Christ's love has the power to change everything, including you.

MORE GREAT IDEAS ABOUT FOLLOWING JESUS

Peter said, "No, Lord!" But he had to learn that one cannot say "No" while saying "Lord" and that one cannot say "Lord" while saying "No."

Corrie ten Boom

We have in Jesus Christ a perfect example of how to put God's truth into practice.

Bill Bright

As we live moment by moment under the control of the Spirit, His character, which is the character of Jesus, becomes evident to those around us.

Anne Graham Lotz

Will you, with a glad and eager surrender, hand yourself and all that concerns you over into his hands? If you will do this, your soul will begin to know something of the joy of union with Christ.

Hannah Whitall Smith

MORE FROM GOD'S WORD

But whoever keeps His word, truly in him the love of God is perfected. This is how we know we are in Him: the one who says he remains in Him should walk just as He walked.

1 John 2:5-6 HCSB

We encouraged, comforted, and implored each one of you to walk worthy of God, who calls you into His own kingdom and glory.

1 Thessalonians 2:12 HCSB

"Follow Me," Jesus told them, "and I will make you into fishers of men!" Immediately they left their nets and followed Him.

Mark 1:17-18 HCSB

The next day John saw Jesus coming toward him and said, "Here is the Lamb of God, who takes away the sin of the world!"

John 1:29 HCSB

A PRAYER FOR TODAY

Dear Jesus, My life has been changed forever by Your love and sacrifice. Today I will praise You, I will honor You, and I will walk with You. Amen

Acquire wisdom—how much better it is than gold! And acquire understanding—it is preferable to silver.

Proverbs 16:16 HCSB

ACQUIRING WISDOM

Proverbs 16:16 teaches us that wisdom is more valuable than gold. All of us would like to be wise, but not all of us are willing to do the work that is required to become wise. Wisdom is not like a mushroom; it does not spring up overnight. It is, instead, like an oak tree that starts as a tiny acorn, grows into a sapling, and eventually reaches up to the sky, tall and strong.

To become wise, we must seek God's wisdom and live according to His Word. To become wise, we must seek wisdom with consistency and purpose. To become wise, we must not only learn the lessons of the Christian life, we must also live by them.

Do you seek to live a life of righteousness and wisdom? If so, you must study the ultimate source of wisdom: the Word of God. You must seek out worthy mentors and listen carefully to their advice. You must associate, day in and day out, with godly men and women. Then, as you accumulate wisdom, you must not keep it for yourself; you must, instead, share it with your friends and family members.

But be forewarned: if you sincerely seek to share your hard-earned wisdom with others, your actions must give credence to your words. The best way to share one's wisdom—perhaps the only way—is not by words, but by example.

MORE GREAT IDEAS ABOUT WISDOM

Wisdom is knowledge applied. Head knowledge is useless on the battlefield. Knowledge stamped on the heart makes one wise.

Beth Moore

If we neglect the Bible, we cannot expect to benefit from the wisdom and direction that result from knowing God's Word.

Vonette Bright

Knowledge can be found in books or in school. Wisdom, on the other hand, starts with God . . . and ends there.

Marie T. Freeman

MORE FROM GOD'S WORD

Above all and before all, do this: Get Wisdom! Write this at the top of your list: Get Understanding!

Proverbs 4:7 MSG

I will instruct you and teach you in the way you should go; I will counsel you and watch over you.

Psalm 32:8 NIV

Those who are wise will shine like the bright expanse [of the heavens], and those who lead many to righteousness, like the stars forever and ever.

Daniel 12:3 HCSB

A PRAYER FOR TODAY

Dear Lord, when I trust in the wisdom of the world, I am often led astray, but when I trust in Your wisdom, I build my life upon a firm foundation. Today and every day I will trust Your Word and follow it, knowing that the ultimate wisdom is Your wisdom and the ultimate truth is Your truth. Amen

But the fruit of the Spirit is love, joy, peace, patience, kindness, goodness, faith, gentleness, self-control. Against such things there is no law.

Galatians 5:22-23 HCSB

THE FRUIT OF THE SPIRIT

In Galatians 5, we are also told that when people live by the Spirit, they will bear "fruit of the Spirit." But what, exactly, is the fruit of the Spirit? It's a way of behaving yourself, a way of treating other people, a way of showing the world what it means to be a Christian. The Bible says, "The fruit of the Spirit is love, joy, peace, patience, kindness, goodness, faith, gentleness, self-control."

Today and every day, will you strive to be patient, joyful, loving, and kind? Will you really try to control yourself? And while you're at it, will you be peaceful, gentle, patient, and faithful? If so, you'll demonstrate to the world that the fruit of the Spirit can make a wonderful difference in the lives of good Christian people—people like you!

MORE GREAT IDEAS ABOUT THE FRUIT OF THE SPIRIT

The Holy Spirit cannot be located as a guest in a house. He invades everything.

Oswald Chambers

Some people have received Christ but have never reached spiritual maturity. We should grow as Christians every day, and we are not completely mature until we live in the presence of Christ.

Billy Graham

The Holy Spirit is like a living and continually flowing fountain in believers. We have the boundless privilege of tapping into that fountain every time we pray.

Shirley Dobson

A PRAYER FOR TODAY

Dear Lord, I know that You sent Jesus to save the world and to save me. Today and every day, help me become the kind of person who always lets Your spirit live and grow in my heart. Amen

These things have I spoken unto you, that my joy might remain in you, and that your joy might be full.

John 15:11 KJV

MAKING HIS JOY YOUR JOY

Christ made it clear: He intends that His joy should become our joy. Yet sometimes, amid the inevitable hustle and bustle of life here on earth, we can forfeit—albeit temporarily—the joy of Christ as we wrestle with the challenges of daily living.

Jonathan Edwards, the 18th-century American clergyman, observed, "Christ is not only a remedy for your weariness and trouble, but he will give you an abundance of the contrary: joy and delight. They who come to Christ do not only come to a resting-place after they have been wandering in a wilderness, but they come to a banqueting-house where they may rest, and where they may feast. They may cease from their former troubles and toils, and they may enter upon a course of delights and spiritual joys."

If, today, your heart is heavy, open the door of your soul to Christ. He will give you peace and joy. And, if you already have the joy of Christ in your heart, share it freely, just as Christ freely shared His joy with you.

More Great Ideas About Joy

Joy is the direct result of having God's perspective on our daily lives and the effect of loving our Lord enough to obey His commands and trust His promises.

Bill Bright

If you can forgive the person you were, accept the person you are, and believe in the person you will become, you are headed for joy. So celebrate your life.

Barbara Johnson

God knows everything. He can manage everything, and He loves us. Surely this is enough for a fullness of joy that is beyond words.

Hannah Whitall Smith

A Prayer for Today

Dear Lord, You have given me so many blessings; let me celebrate Your gifts. Make me thankful, loving, responsible, and wise. I praise You, Father, for the gift of Your Son and for the priceless gift of salvation. Make me be a joyful Christian, a worthy example to others, and a dutiful servant to You this day and forever. Amen

Rejoice in the Lord always. Again I will say, rejoice!

Philippians 4:4 NKJV

REJOICE!

Are you living a life of agitation, consternation, or celebration? If you're a believer, it should most certainly be the latter. With Christ as your Savior, every day should be a time of celebration.

Oswald Chambers correctly observed, "Joy is the great note all throughout the Bible." C. S. Lewis echoed that thought when he wrote, "Joy is the serious business of heaven." But, even the most dedicated Christians can, on occasion, forget to celebrate each day for what it is: a priceless gift from God.

Today, celebrate the life that God has given you. Today, put a smile on your face, kind words on your lips, and a song in your heart. Be generous with your praise and free with your encouragement. And then, when you have celebrated life to the fullest, invite your friends to do likewise. After all, this is God's day, and He has given us clear instructions for its use. We are commanded to rejoice and be glad. So, with no further ado, let the celebration begin.

MORE GREAT IDEAS ABOUT CELEBRATION

If you can forgive the person you were, accept the person you are, and believe in the person you will become, you are headed for joy. So celebrate your life.

Barbara Johnson

Joy is the direct result of having God's perspective on our daily lives and the effect of loving our Lord enough to obey His commands and trust His promises.

Bill Bright

Christ is the secret, the source, the substance, the center, and the circumference of all true and lasting gladness.

Mrs. Charles E. Cowman

A PRAYER FOR TODAY

Dear Lord, You have given me so many reasons to celebrate. Today, let me choose an attitude of cheerfulness. Let me be a joyful Christian, Lord, quick to laugh and slow to anger. And, let me share Your goodness with my family, my friends, and my neighbors, this day and every day. Amen

As the Father loved Me, I also have loved you; abide in My love.

John 15:9 NKJV

CHRIST'S LOVE

How much does Christ love us? More than we, as mere mortals, can comprehend. His love is perfect and steadfast. Even though we are fallible and wayward, the Good Shepherd cares for us still. Even though we have fallen far short of the Father's commandments, Christ loves us with a power and depth that are beyond our understanding. The sacrifice that Jesus made upon the cross was made for each of us, and His love endures to the edge of eternity and beyond.

Hannah Whitall Smith spoke to believers of every generation when she advised, "Keep your face upturned to Christ as the flowers do to the sun. Look, and your soul shall live and grow." How true. When we turn our hearts to Jesus, we receive His blessings, His peace, and His grace.

Christ is the ultimate Savior of mankind and the personal Savior of those who believe in Him. As His servants, we should place Him at the very center of our lives. And, every day that God gives us breath, we should share Christ's love and His message with a world that needs both.

Christ's love changes everything. When you accept His gift of grace, you are transformed, not only for today, but also for all eternity. If you haven't already done so, accept Jesus Christ as your personal Savior. He's waiting patiently for you to invite Him into your heart. Please don't make Him wait a single minute longer.

But God demonstrates His own love toward us, in that while we were still sinners, Christ died for us.

—

Romans 5:8 NKJV

MORE GREAT IDEAS ABOUT CHRIST'S LOVE

Live your lives in love, the same sort of love which Christ gives us, and which He perfectly expressed when He gave Himself as a sacrifice to God.

Corrie ten Boom

No man ever loved like Jesus. He taught the blind to see and the dumb to speak. He died on the cross to save us. He bore our sins. And now God says, "Because He did, I can forgive you."

Billy Graham

Jesus loves me! This I know, for the Bible tells me so. Little ones to him belong; they are weak, but he is strong. / Yes, Jesus loves me! Yes, Jesus loves me! Yes, Jesus loves me! The Bible tells me so.

Anna B. Warner and Susan Warner

A PRAYER FOR TODAY

Dear Jesus, I praise You for Your Love, a love that never ends. Today, I will return Your love and I will share it with the world. Amen

The greatest among you must be a servant. But those who exalt themselves will be humbled, and those who humble themselves will be exalted.

Matthew 23:11-12 NKJV

STAYING HUMBLE

As fallible human beings, we have so much to be humble about. Why, then, is humility such a difficult trait for us to master? Precisely because we are fallible human beings. Yet, if we are to grow and mature as Christians, we must strive to give credit where credit is due, starting, of course, with God and His only begotten Son.

As Christians, we have been refashioned and saved by Jesus Christ, and that salvation came not because of our own good works but because of God's grace. Thus, we are not "self-made"; we are "God-made," and we are "Christ-saved." How, then, can we be boastful? The answer, of course, is that, if we are honest with ourselves and with our God, we simply can't be boastful . . . we must, instead, be eternally grateful and exceedingly humble. Humility, however, is not easy for most of us. All too often, we are tempted to stick out our chests and say, "Look at me; look what I did!" But, in the quiet moments when we search the depths of our own hearts, we know better. Whatever "it" is, God did that. And He deserves the credit.

MORE GREAT IDEAS ABOUT HUMILITY

That's what I love about serving God. In His eyes, there are no little people . . . because there are no big people. We are all on the same playing field. We all start at square one. No one has it better than the other, or possesses unfair advantage.

Joni Eareckson Tada

I can usually sense that a leading is from the Holy Spirit when it calls me to humble myself, to serve somebody, to encourage somebody, or to give something away. Very rarely will the evil one lead us to do those kind of things.

Bill Hybels

A PRAYER FOR TODAY

Heavenly Father, Jesus clothed Himself with humility when He chose to leave heaven and come to earth to live and die for all creation. Christ is my Master and my example. Clothe me with humility, Lord, so that I might be more like Your Son. Amen

Be strong and courageous, and do the work. Do not be afraid or discouraged, for the Lord God, my God, is with you.

1 Chronicles 28:20 NIV

BEYOND THE FEAR OF FAILURE

As we consider the uncertainties of the future, we are confronted with a powerful temptation: the temptation to "play it safe." Unwilling to move mountains, we fret over molehills. Unwilling to entertain great hopes for the tomorrow, we focus on the unfairness of the today. Unwilling to trust God completely, we take timid half-steps when God intends that we make giant leaps.

Today, ask God for the courage to step beyond the boundaries of your doubts. Ask Him to guide you to a place where you can realize your full potential—a place where you are freed from the fear of failure. Ask Him to do His part, and promise Him that you will do your part. Don't ask Him to lead you to a "safe" place; ask Him to lead you to the "right" place . . . and remember: those two places are seldom the same.

MORE GREAT IDEAS ABOUT THE FEAR OF FAILURE

Risk must be taken because the greatest hazard in life is to risk nothing.

John Maxwell

With each new experience of letting God be in control, we gain courage and reinforcement for daring to do it again and again.

Gloria Gaither

Only a person who dares to risk is free.

Joey Johnson

Do not be one of those who, rather than risk failure, never attempt anything.

Thomas Merton

A PRAYER FOR TODAY

Dear Lord, even when I'm afraid of failure, give me the courage to try. Remind me that with You by my side, I really have nothing to fear. So today, Father, I will live courageously as I place my faith in You. Amen

Heaven and earth will pass away, but My words will never pass away.

Matthew 24:35 HCSB

TRUST GOD'S WORD

Are you a person who trusts God's Word without reservation? Hopefully so, because the Bible is unlike any other book—it is a guidebook for life here on earth and for life eternal.

As a Christian, you are instructed to study God's Holy Word, to trust His Word, to follow its commandments, and to share its Good News with the world. The Psalmist writes, "Your word is a lamp to my feet and a light to my path" (Psalm 119:105 NASB). Is the Bible your lamp? If not, you are depriving yourself of a priceless gift from the Creator.

Vance Havner observed, "It takes calm, thoughtful, prayerful meditation on the Word to extract its deepest nourishment." How true. God's Word can be a roadmap to a place of righteousness and abundance. Make it your roadmap. God's wisdom can be a light to guide your steps. Claim it as your light today, tomorrow, and every day of your life—and then walk confidently in the footsteps of God's only begotten Son.

MORE GREAT IDEAS ABOUT
GOD'S WORD

Words fail to express my love for this holy Book, my gratitude for its author, for His love and goodness. How shall I thank him for it?

Lottie Moon

For whatever life holds for you and your family in the coming days, weave the unfailing fabric of God's Word through your heart and mind. It will hold strong, even if the rest of life unravels.

Gigi Graham Tchividjian

God can see clearly no matter how dark or foggy the night is. Trust His Word to guide you safely home.

Lisa Whelchel

A PRAYER FOR TODAY

Heavenly Father, Your Holy Word is a light unto the world; let me study it, trust it, and share it with all who cross my path. In all that I do, help me be a worthy witness for You as I share the Good News of Your perfect Son and Your perfect Word. Amen

But Jesus looked at them and said to them, "With men this is impossible, but with God all things are possible."

Matthew 19:26 NKJV

ALL THINGS ARE POSSIBLE

Sometimes, because we are imperfect human beings with limited understanding and limited faith, we place limitations on God. But, God's power has no limitations. God will work miracles in our lives if we trust Him with everything we have and everything we are. When we do, we experience the miraculous results of His endless love and His awesome power.

Miracles, both great and small, are an integral part of everyday life, but usually, we are too busy or too cynical to notice God's handiwork. We don't expect to see miracles, so we simply overlook them.

Do you lack the faith that God can work miracles in your own life? If so, it's time to reconsider. If you have allowed yourself to become a "doubting Thomas," you are attempting to place limitations on a God who has none. Instead of doubting your Heavenly Father, you must trust Him. Then, you must wait and watch . . . because something miraculous is going to happen to you, and it might just happen today.

MORE GREAT IDEAS ABOUT MIRACLES

There is Someone who makes possible what seems completely impossible.

Catherine Marshall

When we face an impossible situation, all self-reliance and self-confidence must melt away; we must be totally dependent on Him for the resources.

Anne Graham Lotz

Here lies the tremendous mystery—that God should be all-powerful, yet refuse to coerce. He summons us to cooperation. We are honored in being given the opportunity to participate in His good deeds. Remember how He asked for help in performing His miracles: Fill the water pots, stretch out your hand, distribute the loaves.

Elisabeth Elliot

A PRAYER FOR TODAY

Dear Lord, keep me always mindful of Your strength. When I lose hope, give me faith; when others lose hope, let me tell them of Your glory and Your works. Because nothing is impossible for You, I will pray for miracles . . . and I will work for them. Amen

Make a joyful noise unto the LORD, all ye lands. Serve the LORD with gladness: come before his presence with singing.

Psalm 100:1-2 KJV

MAKE A JOYFUL NOISE

When is the best time to "make a joyful noise" by praising God? In church? Before dinner is served? When we tuck little children into bed? None of the above. The best time to praise God is all day, every day, to the greatest extent we can, with thanksgiving in our hearts and with a song on our lips.

Too many of us, even well-intentioned believers, tend to compartmentalize our waking hours into a few familiar categories: work, rest, play, family time, and worship. To do so is a mistake. Worship and praise should be woven into the fabric of everything we do; it should never be relegated to a weekly three-hour visit to church on Sunday morning.

Theologian Wayne Oates once admitted, "Many of my prayers are made with my eyes open. You see, it seems I'm always praying about something, and it's not always convenient—or safe—to close my eyes." Dr. Oates understood that God always hears our prayers and that the relative position of our eyelids is of no concern to Him.

Today, find a little more time to lift your concerns to God in prayer, and praise Him for all that He has done. Whether your eyes are open or closed, He's listening.

MORE GREAT IDEAS ABOUT JOY

He wants us to have a faith that does not complain while waiting, but rejoices because we know our times are in His hands—nail-scarred hands that labor for our highest good.

Kay Arthur

Gratitude changes the pangs of memory into a tranquil joy.

Dietrich Bonhoeffer

Where the soul is full of peace and joy, outward surroundings and circumstances are of comparatively little account.

Hannah Whitall Smiith

Our God is so wonderfully good, and lovely, and blessed in every way that the mere fact of belonging to Him is enough for an untellable fullness of joy!

Hannah Whitall Smith

MORE FROM GOD'S WORD

Praise the Lord, all nations! Glorify Him, all peoples! For great is His faithful love to us; the Lord's faithfulness endures forever. Hallelujah!

Psalm 117 HCSB

But I will hope continually and will praise You more and more.

Psalm 71:14 HCSB

So that at the name of Jesus every knee should bow—of those who are in heaven and on earth and under the earth—and every tongue should confess that Jesus Christ is Lord, to the glory of God the Father.

Philippians 2:10-11 HCSB

A PRAYER FOR TODAY

Heavenly Father, I come to You today with hope in my heart and praise on my lips. Make me a faithful steward of the blessings You have entrusted to me. Let me follow in Christ's footsteps today and every day that I live. And let my words and deeds praise You now and forever. Amen

But those who wait on the Lord shall renew their strength; they shall mount up with wings like eagles, they shall run and not be weary, they shall walk and not faint.

Isaiah 40:31 NKJV

STRENGTH FROM GOD

Even the most inspired Christians can, from time to time, find themselves running on empty. The demands of daily life can drain us of our strength and rob us of the joy that is rightfully ours in Christ. When we find ourselves tired, discouraged, or worse, there is a source from which we can draw the power needed to recharge our spiritual batteries. That source is God.

God intends that His children lead joyous lives filled with abundance and peace. But sometimes, abundance and peace seem very far away. It is then that we must turn to God for renewal, and when we do, He will restore us if we allow Him to do so.

Today, like every other day, is literally brimming with possibilities. Whether we realize it or not, God is always working in us and through us; our job is to let Him do His work without undue interference. Yet we are imperfect beings who, because of our limited vision, often resist God's will. And oftentimes, because of our stubborn insistence on squeezing too many activities into a 24-hour day, we allow ourselves to become exhausted, or frustrated, or both.

Are you tired or troubled? Turn your heart toward God in prayer. Are you weak or worried? Take the time—or, more accurately, make the time—to delve deeply into God's Holy Word. Are you spiritually depleted? Call upon fellow believers to support you, and call upon Christ to renew your spirit and your life. Are you simply overwhelmed by the demands of the day? Pray for the wisdom to simplify your life. Are you exhausted? Pray for the wisdom to rest a little more and worry a little less.

When you do these things, you'll discover that the Creator of the universe stands always ready and always able to create a new sense of wonderment and joy in you.

You, therefore, my child, be strong in the grace that is in Christ Jesus.

—

2 Timothy 2:1 HCSB

MORE GREAT IDEAS ABOUT STRENGTH

The same God who empowered Samson, Gideon, and Paul seeks to empower my life and your life, because God hasn't changed.

Bill Hybels

No matter how heavy the burden, daily strength is given, so I expect we need not give ourselves any concern as to what the outcome will be. We must simply go forward.

Annie Armstrong

God conquers only what we yield to Him. Yet, when He does, and when our surrender is complete, He fills us with a new strength that we could never have known by ourselves. His conquest is our victory!

Shirley Dobson

A PRAYER FOR TODAY

Dear Lord, I will turn to You for strength. When my responsibilities seem overwhelming, I will trust You to give me courage and perspective. Today and every day, I will look to You as the ultimate source of my hope, my strength, my peace, and my salvation. Amen

I am the vine, you are the branches. He who abides in Me, and I in him, bears much fruit; for without Me you can do nothing.

John 15:5 NKJV

HE IS THE VINE

He was the Son of God, but He wore a crown of thorns. He was the Savior of mankind, yet He was put to death on a roughhewn cross. He offered His healing touch to an unsaved world, and yet the same hands that had healed the sick and raised the dead were pierced with nails.

Jesus Christ, the Son of God, was born into humble circumstances. He walked this earth, not as a ruler of men, but as the Savior of mankind. His crucifixion, a torturous punishment that was intended to end His life and His reign, instead became the pivotal event in the history of all humanity. Christ sacrificed His life on the cross so that we might have eternal life. This gift, freely given by God's only begotten Son, is the priceless possession of everyone who accepts Him as Lord and Savior.

Why did Christ endure the humiliation and torture of the cross? He did it for you. His love is as near as your next breath, as personal as your next thought, more essential than your next heartbeat. And what must you do in response to the Savior's gifts? You must accept His love, praise His name, and share His message of salvation. And, you must conduct yourself in a manner that demonstrates to all the world that your acquaintance with the Master is not a passing fancy but that it is, instead, the cornerstone and the touchstone of your life.

I have come as a light into the world, so that everyone who believes in Me would not remain in darkness.

—

John 12:46 HCSB

MORE GREAT IDEAS ABOUT JESUS

Tell me the story of Jesus. Write on my heart every word. Tell me the story most precious, sweetest that ever was heard.

Fanny Crosby

Jesus was the perfect reflection of God's nature in every situation He encountered during His time here on earth.

Bill Hybels

Jesus makes God visible. But that truth does not make Him somehow less than God. He is equally supreme with God.

Anne Graham Lotz

The crucial question for each of us is this: What do you think of Jesus, and do you yet have a personal acquaintance with Him?

Hannah Whitall Smith

A PRAYER FOR TODAY

Heavenly Father, I praise You for Your Son. Jesus is my Savior and my strength. Let me share His Good News with all who cross my path, and let me share His love with all who need His healing touch. Amen

You will show me the path of life; in Your presence is fullness of joy; at Your right hand are pleasures forevermore.

Psalm 16:11 NKJV

HE WILL SHOW YOU THE PATH

L ife is best lived on purpose. And purpose, like everything else in the universe, begins in the heart of God. Whether you realize it or not, God has a direction for your life, a divine calling, a path along which He intends to lead you. When you welcome God into your heart and establish a genuine relationship with Him, He will begin—and He will continue—to make His purposes known.

Each morning, as the sun rises in the east, you welcome a new day, one that is filled to the brim with opportunities, with possibilities, and with God. As you contemplate God's blessings in your own life, you should prayerfully seek His guidance for the day ahead.

Discovering God's unfolding purpose for your life is a daily journey, a journey guided by the teachings of God's Holy Word. As you reflect upon God's promises and upon the meaning that those promises hold for you, ask God to lead you throughout the coming day. Let your Heavenly Father direct your steps; concentrate on what God wants you to do now, and leave the distant future in hands that are far more capable than your own: His hands.

Sometimes, God's intentions will be clear to you; other times, God's plan will seem uncertain at best. But even on those difficult days when you are unsure which way to turn, you must never lose sight of these overriding facts: God created you for a reason; He has important work for you to do; and He's waiting patiently for you to do it. So why not begin today?

I will instruct you and show you the way to go; with My eye on you, I will give counsel.

—

Psalm 32:8 HCSB

MORE GREAT IDEAS ABOUT LIVING ON PURPOSE

Yesterday is just experience but tomorrow is glistening with purpose—and today is the channel leading from one to the other.

Barbara Johnson

In the very place where God has put us, whatever its limitations, whatever kind of work it may be, we may indeed serve the Lord Christ.

Elisabeth Elliot

Only God's chosen task for you will ultimately satisfy. Do not wait until it is too late to realize the privilege of serving Him in His chosen position for you.

Beth Moore

A PRAYER FOR TODAY

Dear Lord, I know that You have a purpose for my life, and I will seek that purpose today and every day that I live. Let my actions be pleasing to You, and let me share Your Good News with a world that so desperately needs Your healing hand and the salvation of Your Son. Amen

Now by this we know that we know Him, if we keep His commandments.

1 John 2:3 NKJV

OBEDIENCE NOW

Obedience to God is determined not by words, but by deeds. Talking about righteousness is easy; living righteously is far more difficult, especially in today's temptation-filled world.

Since God created Adam and Eve, we human beings have been rebelling against our Creator. Why? Because we are unwilling to trust God's Word, and we are unwilling to follow His commandments. God has given us a guidebook for righteous living called the Holy Bible. It contains thorough instructions which, if followed, lead to fulfillment, abundance, and salvation. But, if we choose to ignore God's commandments, the results are as predictable as they are tragic.

When we seek righteousness in our own lives—and when we seek the companionship of those who do likewise—we reap the spiritual rewards that God intends for our lives. When we behave ourselves as godly men and women, we honor God. When we live righteously and according to God's commandments, He blesses us in ways that we cannot fully understand.

Do you seek God's peace and His blessings? Then obey Him. When you're faced with a difficult choice or a powerful temptation, seek God's counsel and trust the counsel He gives. Invite God into your heart and live according to His commandments. When you do, you will be blessed today, and tomorrow, and forever.

Jesus answered, "If anyone loves Me, he will keep My word. My Father will love him, and We will come to him and make Our home with him."

—

John 14:23 HCSB

MORE GREAT IDEAS ABOUT OBEDIENCE

Believe and do what God says. The life-changing consequences will be limitless, and the results will be confidence and peace of mind.

Franklin Graham

Jesus is Victor. Calvary is the place of victory. Obedience is the pathway of victory. Bible study and prayer is the preparation for victory.

Corrie ten Boom

I don't always like His decisions, but when I choose to obey Him, the act of obedience still "counts" with Him even if I'm not thrilled about it.

Beth Moore

A PRAYER FOR TODAY

Dear Heavenly Father, You have blessed me with a love that is infinite and eternal. Let me demonstrate my love for You by obeying Your commandments. Make me a faithful servant, Father, today and throughout eternity. And, let me show my love for You by sharing Your message and Your love with others. Amen

But seek first the kingdom of God and His righteousness, and all these things shall be added to you. Therefore do not worry about tomorrow, for tomorrow will worry about its own things. Sufficient for the day is its own trouble.

Matthew 6:33-34 NKJV

BEYOND WORRY

Because we are imperfect human beings struggling with imperfect circumstances, we worry. Even though we, as Christians, have the assurance of salvation—even though we, as Christians, have the promise of God's love and protection—we find ourselves fretting over the inevitable frustrations of everyday life. Jesus understood our concerns when He spoke the reassuring words found in the 6th chapter of Matthew.

Where is the best place to take your worries? Take them to God. Take your troubles to Him; take your fears to Him; take your doubts to Him; take your weaknesses to Him; take your sorrows to Him . . . and leave them all there. Seek protection from the One who offers you eternal salvation; build your spiritual house upon the Rock that cannot be moved.

Perhaps you are concerned about your future, your health, or your finances. Or perhaps you are simply a "worrier" by nature. If so, make Matthew 6 a regular part of your daily Bible reading. This beautiful passage will remind you that God still sits in His heaven and you are His beloved child. Then, perhaps, you will worry a little less and trust God a little more, and that's as it should be because God is trustworthy . . . and you are protected.

Don't worry about anything,
but in everything, through prayer
and petition with thanksgiving,
let your requests be made
known to God.

—

Philippians 4:6 HCSB

MORE GREAT IDEAS ABOUT WORRY

Never yield to gloomy anticipation. Place your hope and confidence in God. He has no record of failure.

Mrs. Charles E. Cowman

The beginning of anxiety is the end of faith, and the beginning of true faith is the end of anxiety.

George Mueller

Worry is the senseless process of cluttering up tomorrow's opportunities with leftover problems from today.

Barbara Johnson

We are not called to be burden-bearers, but cross-bearers and light-bearers. We must cast our burdens on the Lord.

Corrie ten Boom

A PRAYER FOR TODAY

Lord, You understand my worries and my fears, and You forgive me when I am weak. When my faith begins to waver, help me to trust You more. Then, with Your Holy Word on my lips and with the love of Your Son in my heart, let me live courageously, faithfully, prayerfully, and thankfully today and every day. Amen

Blessed are the merciful, because they will be shown mercy.

Matthew 5:7 HCSB

BE MERCIFUL

If we wish to build lasting relationships, we must learn how to forgive. Why? Because our loved ones are imperfect (as are we). How often must we forgive our spouses and our friends? More times than we can count; to do otherwise is to disobey God.

Are you easily frustrated by the inevitable imperfections of others? Are you easily angered? Do you sometimes hold on to feelings of bitterness and regret? If so, perhaps you need a refresher course in the art of forgiveness.

Perhaps granting forgiveness is hard for you. If so, you are not alone. Genuine, lasting forgiveness is often difficult to achieve—difficult but not impossible. Thankfully, with God's help, all things are possible, and that includes forgiveness. But even though God is willing to help, He expects you to do some of the work.

If there exists even one person, alive or dead, whom you have not forgiven (and that includes yourself and, of course, your spouse), follow God's commandment and His will for your life: forgive. Bitterness, anger, and regret are not part of God's plan for your life.

MORE GREAT IDEAS ABOUT LOVE AND FORGIVENESS

When God forgives, He forgets. He buries our sins in the sea and puts a sign on the shore saying, "No Fishing Allowed."

Corrie ten Boom

Jesus had a forgiving and understanding heart. If he lives within us, mercy will temper our relationships with our fellow men.

Billy Graham

The more you practice the art of forgiving, the quicker you'll master the art of living.

Marie T. Freeman

God expects us to forgive others as He has forgiven us; we are to follow His example by having a forgiving heart.

Vonette Bright

A PRAYER FOR TODAY

Dear Lord, today I will choose to forgive those who have hurt me. I will empty my heart of bitterness and fill it with love. I will obey Your Word by offering love and mercy to others, just as You have offered mercy and love to me. Amen

Therefore, if anyone is in Christ, he is a new creation; old things have passed away; behold, all things have become new.

2 Corinthians 5:17 NKJV

THE NEW YOU

In 2 Corinthians 5:17, we are told that when a person accepts Christ, he or she becomes a new creation. Have you invited God's Son to reign over your heart and your life? If so, think for a moment about the "old" you, the person you were before you invited Christ into your heart. Now, think about the "new" you, the person you have become since then. Is there a difference between the "old" you and the "new and improved" version? There should be! And that difference should be noticeable not only to you but also to others.

Warren Wiersbe observed, "The greatest miracle of all is the transformation of a lost sinner into a child of God." And Oswald Chambers noted, "If the Spirit of God has transformed you within, you will exhibit Divine characteristics in your life, not good human characteristics. God's life in us expresses itself as God's life, not as a human life trying to be godly."

When you invited Christ to reign over your heart, you become a new creation through Him. This day offers yet another opportunity to behave yourself like that new creation by serving your Creator and strengthening your character. When you do, God will guide your steps and bless your endeavors today and forever.

Therefore we were buried with Him by baptism into death, in order that, just as Christ was raised from the dead by the glory of the Father, so we too may walk in a new way of life.

Romans 6:4 HCSB

MORE GREAT IDEAS ABOUT CONVERSION

God is not a supernatural interferer; God is the everlasting portion of his people. When a man born from above begins his new life, he meets God at every turn, hears him in every sound, sleeps at his feet, and wakes to find him there.

Oswald Chambers

The amazing thing about Jesus is that He doesn't just patch up our lives, He gives us a brand new sheet, a clean slate to start over, all new.

Gloria Gaither

If you are God's child, you are no longer bound to your past or to what you were. You are a brand new creature in Christ Jesus.

Kay Arthur

A PRAYER FOR TODAY

Lord, when I accepted Jesus as my personal Savior, You changed me forever and made me whole. Let me share Your Son's message with my friends, with my family, and with the world. You are a God of love, redemption, conversion, and salvation. I will praise You today and forever. Amen

Blessed are those who hunger and thirst for righteousness, because they will be filled.

Matthew 5:6 HCSB

LIVING RIGHTEOUSLY

Matthew 5:6 teaches us that righteous men and women are blessed. Do you sincerely desire to be a righteous person? Are you bound and determined—despite the inevitable temptations and distractions of our modern age—to be an example of godly behavior to your family, to your friends, to your coworkers, and to your community? If so, you must obey God's commandments. There are no shortcuts and no loopholes—to be a faithful Christian, you must be an obedient Christian.

You will never become righteous by accident. You must hunger for righteousness, and you must ask God to guide your steps. When you ask Him for guidance, He will give it. So, when you're faced with a difficult choice or a powerful temptation, seek God's counsel and trust the counsel He gives. Invite God into your heart and live according to His commandments. When you do, you will be blessed today, tomorrow, and forever.

MORE GREAT IDEAS ABOUT DOING WHAT'S RIGHT

Holiness has never been the driving force of the majority. It is, however, mandatory for anyone who wants to enter the kingdom.

Elisabeth Elliot

Impurity is not just a wrong action; impurity is the state of mind and heart and soul which is just the opposite of purity and wholeness.

A. W. Tozer

He doesn't need an abundance of words. He doesn't need a dissertation about your life. He just wants your attention. He wants your heart.

Kathy Troccoli

A PRAYER FOR TODAY

Holy Father, let my thoughts and my deeds be pleasing to You. I thank You, Lord, for Jesus, the One who took away my sins. Today and every day, I will follow in His footsteps so that my life can be a living testimony to Your love, to Your forgiveness, and to Your Son. Amen

Therefore humble yourselves under the mighty hand of God, that He may exalt you in due time, casting all your care upon Him, for He cares for you.

1 Peter 5:6-7 NKJV

HE CARES

It is easy to become overwhelmed by the demands of everyday life, but if you're a faithful follower of the One from Galilee, you need never be overwhelmed. Why? Because God's love is sufficient to meet your needs. Whatever dangers you may face, whatever heartbreaks you must endure, God is with you, and He stands ready to comfort you and to heal you.

The Psalmist writes, "Weeping may endure for a night, but joy comes in the morning" (Psalm 30:5 NKJV). But when we are suffering, the morning may seem very far away. It is not. God promises that He is "near to those who have a broken heart" (Psalm 34:18 NKJV).

If you are experiencing the intense pain of a recent loss, or if you are still mourning a loss from long ago, perhaps you are now ready to begin the next stage of your journey with God. If so, be mindful of this fact: the loving heart of God is sufficient to meet any challenge, including yours.

MORE GREAT IDEAS ABOUT GOD'S SUPPORT

We have ample evidence that the Lord is able to guide. The promises cover every imaginable situation. All we need to do is to take the hand he stretches out.

Elisabeth Elliot

God uses our most stumbling, faltering faith-steps as the open door to His doing for us "more than we ask or think."

Catherine Marshall

Snuggle in God's arms. When you are hurting, when you feel lonely or left out, let Him cradle you, comfort you, reassure you of His all-sufficient power and love.

Kay Arthur

A PRAYER FOR TODAY

Lord, You have promised never to leave me or forsake me. You are always with me, protecting me and encouraging me. Whatever this day may bring, I thank You for Your love and for Your strength. Let me lean upon You, Father, this day and forever. Amen

Beloved, if God so loved us, we also ought to love one another.

1 John 4:11 NKJV

LOVE ONE ANOTHER

Genuine love requires patience and perseverance. Sometimes we are sorely tempted to treat love as if it were a sprint (which it is not). Genuine love is always a marathon, and those who expect it to be otherwise will always be disappointed.

Building lasting relationships requires a steadfast determination to endure, and as an example of perfect perseverance, we need look no further than our Savior, Jesus Christ. Jesus finished what He began. Despite the torture He endured, despite the shame of the cross, Jesus was steadfast in His faithfulness to God. We, too, must remain faithful in our relationships, especially during times of transition or hardship.

The next time you are tempted to "give up" on a relationship, ask yourself this question: "What would our Savior do?" When you find the answer to that question, you will know precisely what you should do.

MORE GREAT IDEAS ABOUT LOVE

To have fallen in love hints to our hearts that all of earthly life is not hopelessly fallen. Love is the laughter of God.

Beth Moore

The world does not understand theology or dogma, but it does understand love and sympathy.

D. L. Moody

Real love has staying power. Authentic love is tough love. It refuses to look for ways to run away. It always opts for working through.

Charles Swindoll

For love to be true, it sometimes has to be velvet and sometimes it has to be steel.

Charles Stanley

A PRAYER FOR TODAY

Dear Lord, You have given me the gift of love; let me share that gift with others. And, keep me mindful that the essence of love is not to receive it, but to give it, today and forever. Amen

Finally, brethren, whatever things are true, whatever things are noble, whatever things are just, whatever things are pure, whatever things are lovely, whatever things are of good report, if there is any virtue and if there is anything praiseworthy— meditate on these things.

Philippians 4:8 NKJV

THE DIRECTION OF YOUR THOUGHTS

How will you direct your thoughts today? Will you obey the words of Philippians 4:8 by dwelling upon those things that are true, noble, and just? Or will you allow your thoughts to be hijacked by the negativity that seems to dominate our troubled world?

Are you fearful, angry, bored, or worried? Are you so preoccupied with the concerns of this day that you fail to thank God for the promise of eternity? Are you confused, bitter, or pessimistic? If so, God wants to have a little talk with you.

God intends that you be an ambassador for Him, an enthusiastic, hope-filled Christian. But God won't force you to adopt a positive attitude. It's up to you to do think positively about your blessings and opportunities . . . or not. So, today and every day hereafter, celebrate this life that God has given you by focusing your thoughts and your energies upon "things that are excellent and worthy of praise." Today, count your blessings instead of your hardships. And thank the Giver of all things good for gifts that are simply too numerous to count.

May the words of my mouth and the meditation of my heart be acceptable to You, Lord, my rock and my Redeemer.

—

Psalm 19:14 HCSB

MORE GREAT IDEAS ABOUT YOUR THOUGHTS

Attitude is the mind's paintbrush; it can color any situation.

Barbara Johnson

I became aware of one very important concept I had missed before: my attitude—not my circumstances—was what was making me unhappy.

Vonette Bright

Whether we think of, or speak to, God, whether we act or suffer for him, all is prayer when we have no other object than his love and the desire of pleasing him.

John Wesley

A PRAYER FOR TODAY

Dear Lord, keep my thoughts focused on Your love, Your power, Your Promises, and Your Son. When I am worried, I will turn to You for comfort; when I am weak, I will turn to You for strength; when I am troubled, I will turn to You for patience and perspective. Help me guard my thoughts, Father, so that I may honor You today and every day that I live. Amen

I have come as a light into the world, that whoever believes in Me should not abide in darkness.

John 12:46 NKJV

JESUS IS THE LIGHT

The words of John 12:46 teach us that Jesus is the light of the world. And, John 14:6-7 instructs us that Jesus is, "the way, the truth, and the life." Without Christ, we are as far removed from salvation as the east is removed from the west. And without Christ, we can never know the ultimate truth: God's truth.

Truth is God's way: He commands His believers to live in truth, and He rewards those who do so. Jesus is the personification of God's liberating truth, a truth that offers salvation to mankind.

Do you seek to walk with God? Do you seek to feel His presence and His peace? Then you must walk in truth; you must walk in the light; you must walk with the Savior. There is simply no other way.

MORE GREAT IDEAS ABOUT JESUS

There was One, who for "us sinners and our salvation," left the glories of heaven and sojourned upon this earth in weariness and woe, amid those who hated his and finally took his life.

Lottie Moon

I am truly happy with Jesus Christ. I couldn't live without Him. When my life gets beyond the ability to cope, He takes over.

Ruth Bell Graham

Christians see sin for what it is: willful rebellion against the rulership of God in their lives. And in turning from their sin, they have embraced God's only means of dealing with sin: Jesus.

Kay Arthur

A PRAYER FOR TODAY

Heavenly Father, I praise You for Your Son Jesus, the light of the world and my personal Savior. Let me share His Good News with all who cross my path, and let me share His love with all who need His healing touch. Amen

Weeping may endure for a night, but joy comes in the morning.

Psalm 30:5 NKJV

BEYOND GRIEF

Grief visits all of us who live long and love deeply. When we lose a loved one, or when we experience any other profound loss, darkness overwhelms us for a while, and it seems as if our purpose for living has vanished. Thankfully, God has other plans.

The Christian faith, as communicated through the words of the Holy Bible, is a healing faith. It offers comfort in times of trouble, courage for our fears, hope instead of hopelessness. For Christians, the grave is not a final resting-place, it is a place of transition. Through the healing words of God's promises, Christians understand that the Lord continues to manifest His plan in good times and bad.

God intends that you have a meaningful, abundant life, but He expects you to do your part in claiming those blessings. So, as you work through your grief, you will find it helpful to utilize all the resources that God has placed along your path. God makes help available, but it's up to you to find it and then to accept it.

If you are experiencing the intense pain of a recent loss, or if you are still mourning a loss from long ago, perhaps you are now ready to begin the next stage of your journey with God. If so, be mindful of this fact: As a wounded survivor, you will have countless opportunities to serve others. And by serving others, you will bring purpose and meaning to the suffering you've endured.

I have heard your prayer;
I have seen your tears.
Look, I will heal you.

—

2 Kings 20:5 HCSB

MORE GREAT IDEAS ABOUT OVERCOMING GRIEF

There is no way around suffering. We have to go through it to get to the other side.

Barbara Johnson

You learn your theology most where your sorrows take you.

Martin Luther

God's Word never said we were not to grieve our losses. It says we are not to grieve as those who have no hope (1 Thessalonians 4:13). Big Difference.

Beth Moore

There is no pit so deep that God's love is not deeper still.

Corrie ten Boom

A PRAYER FOR TODAY

Heavenly Father, Your Word promises that You will not give us more than we can bear; You have promised to lift us out of our grief and despair. Today, Lord, I pray for those who mourn, and I thank You for sustaining all of us in our days of sorrow. May we trust You always and praise You forever. Amen

Jesus said to him, "'You shall love the Lord your God with all your heart, with all your soul, and with all your mind.' This is the first and great commandment."

Matthew 22:37-38 NKJV

LOVING GOD

C hrist's words are unambiguous: "Love the Lord your God with all your heart and with all your soul and with all your mind." But sometimes, despite our best intentions, we fall short of God's plan for our lives when we become embittered with ourselves, with our neighbors, or most especially with our Creator.

If we are to please God, we must cleanse ourselves of the negative feelings that separate us from others and from Him. In 1 Corinthians 13, we are told that love is the foundation upon which all our relationships are to be built: our relationships with others and our relationship with our Maker.

So today and every day, fill your heart with love; never yield to bitterness; and praise the Son of God who, in His infinite wisdom, made love His greatest commandment.

MORE GREAT IDEAS ABOUT LOVING GOD

I love Him because He first loved me, and He still does love me, and He will love me forever and ever.

Bill Bright

Joy is a by-product not of happy circumstances, education or talent, but of a healthy relationship with God and a determination to love Him no matter what.

Barbara Johnson

God is so inconceivably good. He's not looking for perfection. He already saw it in Christ. He's looking for affection.

Beth Moore

A PRAYER FOR TODAY

Dear Heavenly Father, You have blessed me with a love that is infinite and eternal. Let me love You, Lord, more and more each day. Make me a loving servant, Father, today and throughout eternity. And, let me show my love for You by sharing Your message and Your love with others. Amen

Do not fear, for I am with you; do not be afraid, for I am your God. I will strengthen you; I will help you; I will hold on to you with My righteous right hand.

Isaiah 41:10 HCSB

ABOVE AND BEYOND FEAR

We live in a fear-based world, a world where bad news travels at light speed and good news doesn't. These are troubled times, times when we have legitimate fears for the future of our nation, our world, and our families. But we also have every reason to live courageously. After all, since God has promised to love us and protect us, who—or what—should we fear?

Perhaps you, like countless others, have found your courage tested by the anxieties and fears that are an inevitable part of life. If so, let the words of Isaiah 41:10 serve as a reminder that God wants to you to think less about your challenges and more about His love. Remember that He is not just near, He is here, and He's ready to help right. God will comfort you if you ask Him to. So why not ask? And why now?

MORE GREAT IDEAS ABOUT FEAR

Only believe, don't fear. Our Master, Jesus, always watches over us, and no matter what the persecution, Jesus will surely overcome it.

Lottie Moon

Courage faces fear and thereby masters it. Cowardice represses fear and is thereby mastered by it.

Martin Luther King, Jr.

When once we are assured that God is good, then there can be nothing left to fear.

Hannah Whitall Smith

Fear and doubt are conquered by a faith that rejoices. And faith can rejoice because the promises of God are as certain as God Himself.

Kay Arthur

A PRAYER FOR TODAY

Dear Lord, when I am fearful, keep me mindful that You are my protector and my salvation. Thank You, Father, for a perfect love that casts out fear. Because of You, I can live courageously and faithfully this day and every day. Amen

God is our refuge and strength, a very present help in trouble.

Psalm 46:1 NKJV

GOD IS OUR REFUGE

The words of Psalm 46:1 promise that God is our refuge, a refuge that we all need. From time to time, all of us face adversity, discouragement, or disappointment. And throughout life, we all must endure life-changing personal losses that leave us breathless. When we do, God stands ready to protect us. Psalm 147 assures us that, "He heals the brokenhearted, and binds their wounds" (v. 3, NIV).

Are you anxious? Take those anxieties to God. Are you troubled? Take your troubles to Him. Does the world seem to be trembling beneath your feet? Seek protection from the One who cannot be moved.

The same God who created the universe stands ready and willing to comfort you and to restore your strength. During life's most difficult days, your Heavenly Father remains steadfast. And, in His own time and according to His master plan, He will heal you if you invite Him into your heart.

MORE GREAT IDEAS ABOUT TOUGH TIMES

If all struggles and sufferings were eliminated, the spirit would no more reach maturity than would the child.

Elisabeth Elliot

The sermon of your life in tough times ministers to people more powerfully than the most eloquent speaker.

Bill Bright

Faith is a strong power, mastering any difficulty in the strength of the Lord who made heaven and earth.

Corrie ten Boom

Measure the size of the obstacles against the size of God.

Beth Moore

A PRAYER FOR TODAY

Dear Lord, in the dark moments of my life, help me to remember that You, my Savior, are always near and that You can overcome any challenge. Keep me mindful of Your love and Your power, so that I may live courageously and faithfully today and every day. Amen

Trust in the Lord with all your heart, and lean not on your own understanding; in all your ways acknowledge Him, and He shall direct your paths.

Proverbs 3:5-6 NKJV

TRUST HIM

It's easy to talk about trusting God, but when it comes to actually trusting Him, that's considerably harder. Why? Because genuine trust in God requires more than words; it requires a willingness to follow God's lead and a willingness to obey His commandments. (These, by the way, are not easy things to do.)

Have you spent more time talking about Christ than walking in His footsteps? If so, God wants to have a little chat with you. And, if you're unwilling to talk to Him, He may take other actions in order to grab your attention.

Thankfully, whenever you're willing to talk with God, He's willing to listen. And, the instant that you decide to place Him squarely in the center of your life, He will respond to that decision with blessings that are too unexpected to predict and too numerous to count.

The next time you find your courage tested to the limit, lean upon God's promises. Trust His Son.

Remember that God is always near and that He is your protector and your deliverer. When you are worried, anxious, or afraid, call upon Him. God can handle your troubles infinitely better than you can, so turn them over to Him. Remember that God rules both mountain-tops and valleys—with limitless wisdom and love—now and forever.

The one who understands a matter finds success, and the one who trusts in the Lord will be happy.

—

Proverbs 16:20 HCSB

MORE GREAT IDEAS ABOUT TRUSTING GOD

A prayerful heart and an obedient heart will learn, very slowly and not without sorrow, to stake everything on God Himself.

Elisabeth Elliot

God is God. He knows what he is doing. When you can't trace his hand, trust his heart.

Max Lucado

Sometimes the very essence of faith is trusting God in the midst of things He knows good and well we cannot comprehend.

Beth Moore

A PRAYER FOR TODAY

Dear Lord, I come to You today with hope in my heart and praise on my lips. I place my trust in You, Dear God, knowing that with You as my Protector, I have nothing to fear. I thank You, Father, for Your grace, for Your Love, and for Your Son. Let me follow in Christ's footsteps today and every day that I live. And then, when my work here is done, let me live with You forever. Amen

*Even though I walk through the valley of the shadow of death,
I will fear no evil, for you are with me; your rod and your
staff, they comfort me.*

Psalm 23:4 NIV

TRUST THE SHEPHERD

In the 23rd Psalm, David teaches us that God is like a watchful shepherd caring for His flock. No wonder these verses have provided comfort and hope for generations of believers.

You are precious in the eyes of God. You are His priceless creation, made in His image, and protected by Him. God watches over every step you make and every breath you take, so you need never be afraid. But sometimes, fear has a way of slipping into the minds and hearts of even the most devout believers—and you are no exception.

You know from firsthand experience that life is not always easy. But as a recipient of God's grace, you also know that you are protected by a loving Heavenly Father.

On occasion, you will confront circumstances that trouble you to the very core of your soul. When you are afraid, trust in God. When you are worried, turn your concerns over to Him. When you are anxious, be still and listen for the quiet assurance of God's promises. And then, place your life in His hands. He is your shepherd today and throughout eternity. Trust the Shepherd.

Therefore don't worry about tomorrow, because tomorrow will worry about itself. Each day has enough trouble of its own.

—

Matthew 6:34 HCSB

MORE GREAT IDEAS ABOUT GOD'S COMFORT

We all go through pain and sorrow, but the presence of God, like a warm, comforting blanket, can shield us and protect us, and allow the deep inner joy to surface, even in the most devastating circumstances.

Barbara Johnson

When I am criticized, injured, or afraid, there is a Father who is ready to comfort me.

Max Lucado

Put your hand into the hand of God. He gives the calmness and serenity of heart and soul.

Mrs. Charles E. Cowman

When God allows extraordinary trials for His people, He prepares extraordinary comforts for them.

Corrie ten Boom

A PRAYER FOR TODAY

Dear Lord, thank You for Your comfort. You lift me up when I am disappointed. You protect me in times of trouble. Today, I will be mindful of Your love, Your wisdom, and Your grace. Amen

And now abide faith, hope, love, these three; but the greatest of these is love.

1 Corinthians 13:13 NKJV

THE GREATEST OF THESE IS LOVE

The familiar words of 1st Corinthians 13 remind us of the importance of love. Faith is important, of course. So, too, is hope. But love is more important still.

Christ showed His love for us on the cross, and, as Christians, we are called upon to return Christ's love by sharing it. We are commanded (not advised, not encouraged...commanded!) to love one another just as Christ loved us (John 13:34). That's a tall order, but as Christians, we are obligated to follow it.

Sometimes love is easy (puppies and sleeping children come to mind) and sometimes love is hard (fallible human beings come to mind). But God's Word is clear: We are to love all our friends and neighbors, not just the lovable ones. So today, take time to spread Christ's message by word and by example. And the greatest of these is, of course, is example.

MORE GREAT IDEAS ABOUT LOVE

Love is an attribute of God. To love others is evidence of a genuine faith.

Kay Arthur

He who is filled with love is filled with God Himself.

St. Augustine

Those who abandon ship the first time it enters a storm miss the calm beyond. And the rougher the storms weathered together, the deeper and stronger real love grows.

Ruth Bell Graham

Love is the seed of all hope. It is the enticement to trust, to risk, to try, and to go on.

Gloria Gaither

A PRAYER FOR TODAY

Lord, love is Your commandment. Help me always to remember that the gift of love is a precious gift indeed. Let me nurture love and treasure it. And, keep me mindful that the essence of love is not to receive it, but to give it, today and forever. Amen

Unless the Lord builds a house, its builders labor over it in vain; unless the Lord watches over a city, the watchman stays alert in vain.

Psalm 127:1 HCSB

HE WATCHES OVER US

Have you ever faced challenges that seemed too big to handle? Have you ever faced big problems that, despite your best efforts, simply could not be solved? If so, you know how uncomfortable it is to feel helpless in the face of difficult circumstances. Thankfully, even when there's nowhere else to turn, you can turn your thoughts and prayers to God, and He will respond.

God's hand uplifts those who turn their hearts and prayers to Him. Count yourself among that number. When you do, you can live courageously and joyfully, knowing that "this too will pass"—but that God's love for you will not. And you can draw strength from the knowledge that you are a marvelous creation, loved, protected, and uplifted by the ever-present hand of God.

MORE GREAT IDEAS ABOUT
GOD'S PROTECTION

When you fall and skin your knees and skin your heart, He'll pick you up.

Charles Stanley

Gather the riches of God's promises which can strengthen you in the time when there will be no freedom.

Corrie ten Boom

Trials are not enemies of faith but opportunities to reveal God's faithfulness.

Barbara Johnson

A PRAYER FOR TODAY

Lord, sometimes life is difficult. Sometimes, I am worried, weary, or heartbroken. And sometimes, I encounter powerful temptations to disobey Your commandments. But, when I lift my eyes to You, Father, You strengthen me. When I am weak, You lift me up. Today, I will turn to You for strength, for hope, for direction, and for deliverance. Amen

If you have faith as a mustard seed, you will say to this mountain, "Move from here to there," and it will move; and nothing will be impossible for you.

Matthew 17:20 NKJV

MOUNTAIN-MOVING FAITH

Because we live in a demanding world, all of us have mountains to climb and mountains to move. Moving those mountains requires faith.

Are you a mountain mover whose faith is evident for all to see? Or, are you a spiritual shrinking violet? God needs more men and women who are willing to move mountains for His glory and for His kingdom.

Jesus taught His disciples that if they had faith, they could move mountains. You can too. When you place your faith, your trust, indeed your life in the hands of Christ Jesus, you'll be amazed at the marvelous things He can do. So strengthen your faith through praise, through worship, through Bible study, and through prayer. And trust God's plans. With Him, all things are possible, and He stands ready to open a world of possibilities to you . . . if you have faith.

Concentration camp survivor Corrie ten Boom relied on faith during her long months of imprisonment and torture. Later, despite the fact that four of her family members had died in Nazi death camps, Corrie's faith was unshaken. She wrote, "There is no pit so deep that God's love is not deeper still." Christians take note: Genuine faith in God means faith in all circumstances, happy or sad, joyful or tragic.

If your faith is being tested to the point of breaking, remember that your Savior is near. If you reach out to Him in faith, He will give you peace and strength. Reach out today. If you touch even the smallest fragment of the Master's garment, He will make you whole. And then, with no further ado, let the mountain moving begin.

Jesus said, "Because you have seen Me, you have believed. Blessed are those who believe without seeing."

—

John 20:29 HCSB

MORE GREAT IDEAS ABOUT FAITH

Grace calls you to get up, throw off your blanket of helplessness, and to move on through life in faith.

Kay Arthur

There are a lot of things in life that are difficult to understand. Faith allows the soul to go beyond what the eyes can see.

John Maxwell

Faith is seeing light with the eyes of your heart, when the eyes of your body see only darkness.

Barbara Johnson

Just as our faith strengthens our prayer life, so do our prayers deepen our faith. Let us pray often, starting today, for a deeper, more powerful faith.

Shirley Dobson

A PRAYER FOR TODAY

Lord, as I take the next steps on my life's journey, I will take them with You. Because of my faith in You, I can be courageous and strong. I will lean upon You, Father—and trust you—this day and forever. Amen

To everything there is a season, a time for every purpose under heaven.

Ecclesiastes 3:1 NKJV

TRUST GOD'S TIMING

Sometimes, the hardest thing to do is to wait. This is especially true when we're in a hurry and when we want things to happen now, if not sooner! But God's plan does not always happen in the way that we would like or at the time of our own choosing. Our task—as thoughtful men and women who trust in a benevolent, all-knowing Father—is to wait patiently for God to reveal Himself.

We humans know precisely what we want, and we know exactly when we want it. But, God has a far better plan for each of us. He has created a world that unfolds according to His own timetable, not ours . . . thank goodness! And if we're wise, we trust Him and we wait patiently for Him. After all, He is trustworthy, and He always knows best.

MORE GREAT IDEAS ABOUT GOD'S TIMING

God does not promise to keep us out of the storms and floods, but He does promise to sustain us in the storm, and then bring us out in due time for His glory when the storm has done its work.

Warren Wiersbe

When we read of the great Biblical leaders, we see that it was not uncommon for God to ask them to wait, not just a day or two, but for years, until God was ready for them to act.

Gloria Gaither

God's delays and His ways can be confusing because the process God uses to accomplish His will can go against human logic and common sense.

Anne Graham Lotz

A PRAYER FOR TODAY

Dear Lord, Your timing is seldom my timing, but Your timing is always right for me. You are my Father, and You have a plan for my life that is grander than I can imagine. When I am impatient, remind me that You are never early or late. You are always on time, Lord, so let me trust in You . . . always. Amen

Be still, and know that I am God....

Psalm 46:10 KJV

BE STILL

We live in a noisy world, a world filled with distractions, frustrations, obligations, and complications. But we must not allow our clamorous world to separate us from God's peace. Instead, we must "be still" so that we might sense the presence of God.

If we are to maintain righteous minds and compassionate hearts, we must take time each day for prayer and for meditation. We must make ourselves still in the presence of our Creator. We must quiet our minds and our hearts so that we might sense God's love, God's will, and God's Son.

Has the busy pace of life robbed you of the peace that might otherwise be yours through Jesus Christ? If so, it's time to reorder your priorities. Nothing is more important than the time you spend with your Savior. So be still and claim the inner peace that is your spiritual birthright: the peace of Jesus Christ. It is offered freely; it has been paid for in full; it is yours for the asking. So ask. And then share.

MORE GREAT IDEAS ABOUT QUIET TIME

I don't see how any Christian can survive, let alone live life as more than a conqueror, apart from a quiet time alone with God.

Kay Arthur

Since the quiet hour spent with God is the preacher's power-house, the devil centers his attention on that source of strength.

Vance Havner

The manifold rewards of a serious, consistent prayer life demonstrate clearly that time with our Lord should be our first priority.

Shirley Dobson

In the center of a hurricane there is absolute quiet and peace. There is no safer place than in the center of the will of God.

Corrie ten Boom

A PRAYER FOR TODAY

Dear Lord, help me remember the importance of silence. Help me discover quiet moments throughout the day so that I can sense Your presence and Your love. Amen

So teach us to number our days, that we may gain a heart of wisdom.

Psalm 90:12 NKJV

THE GIFT OF LIFE

Life is a glorious gift from God. Treat it that way.

This day, like every other, is filled to the brim with opportunities, challenges, and choices. But, no choice that you make is more important than the choice you make concerning God. Today, you will either place Him at the center of your life—or not—and the consequences of that choice have implications that are both temporal and eternal.

Sometimes, we don't intentionally neglect God; we simply allow ourselves to become overwhelmed with the demands of everyday life. And then, without our even realizing it, we gradually drift away from the One we need most. Thankfully, God never drifts away from us. God remains always present, always steadfast, always loving.

As you begin this day, place God and His Son where they belong: in your head, in your prayers, on your lips, and in your heart. And then, with God as your guide and companion, let the journey begin . . .

MORE GREAT IDEAS ABOUT LIFE

As I contemplate all the sacrifices required in order to live a life that is totally focused on Jesus Christ and His eternal kingdom, the joy seeps out of my heart onto my face in a smile of deep satisfaction.

Anne Graham Lotz

You have a glorious future in Christ! Live every moment in His power and love.

Vonette Bright

Your life is not a boring stretch of highway. It's a straight line to heaven. And just look at the fields ripening along the way. Look at the tenacity and endurance. Look at the grains of righteousness. You'll have quite a crop at harvest…so don't give up!

Joni Eareckson Tada

A PRAYER FOR TODAY

Lord, You are the Giver of all life. Let me live a life that pleases You, and let me thank You always for Your blessings. You love me and protect me, Heavenly Father. Let me be grateful, and let me live for You today and throughout eternity. Amen

Do not love the world or the things in the world. If anyone loves the world, the love of the Father is not in him.

1 John 2:15 NKJV

THE WORLD'S TREASURES OR GOD'S TREASURES?

All of mankind is engaged in a colossal, worldwide treasure hunt. Some folks seek treasure from earthly sources, treasures such as material wealth or public acclaim; others seek God's treasures by making Him the cornerstone of their lives.

What kind of treasure hunter are you? Are you so caught up in the demands of popular society that you sometimes allow the search for worldly treasures to become your primary focus? If so, it's time to reorganize your daily to-do list by placing God in His rightful place: first place.

If you sincerely seek to strengthen your character, you'll focus more intently on God's treasures and less intently on the world's treasures. Don't allow anyone or anything to separate you from your Heavenly Father and His only begotten Son.

Society's priorities are transitory; God's priorities are permanent. The world's treasures are difficult to find and difficult to keep; God's treasures are ever-present and everlasting. Which treasures and whose priorities will you claim as your own? The answer should be obvious.

MORE GREAT IDEAS ABOUT WORLDLINESS

All those who look to draw their satisfaction from the wells of the world—pleasure, popularity, position, possessions, politics, power, prestige, finances, family, friends, fame, fortune, career, children, church, clubs, sports, sex, success, recognition, reputation, religion, education, entertainment, exercise, honors, health, hobbies—will soon be thirsty again!

Anne Graham Lotz

Our fight is not against any physical enemy; it is against organizations and powers that are spiritual. We must struggle against sin all our lives, but we are assured we will win.

Corrie ten Boom

The more we stuff ourselves with material pleasures, the less we seem to appreciate life.

Barbara Johnson

MORE FROM GOD'S WORD

For whatever is born of God overcomes the world. And this is the victory that has overcome the world—our faith.

1 John 5:4 NKJV

Therefore, come out from among them and be separate, says the Lord; do not touch any unclean thing, and I will welcome you.

2 Corinthians 6:17 HCSB

Set your minds on what is above, not on what is on the earth.

Colossians 3:2 HCSB

And with many other words he testified and strongly urged them, saying, "Be saved from this corrupt generation!"

Acts 2:40 HCSB

A PRAYER FOR TODAY

Dear Lord, I am an imperfect human being living in an imperfect world. Direct my path far from the temptations and distractions of this world, and let me follow in the footsteps of Your Son today and forever. Amen

I have set before you life and death, blessing and curse. Choose life so that you and your descendants may live, love the Lord your God, obey Him, and remain faithful to Him. For He is your life, and He will prolong your life in the land the Lord swore to give to your fathers Abraham, Isaac, and Jacob.

Deuteronomy 30:19-20 HCSB

MAKING GOOD CHOICES

L ife is a series of choices. From the instant we wake in the morning until the moment we nod off to sleep at night, we make countless decisions: decisions about the things we do, decisions about the words we speak, and decisions about the thoughts we choose to think. Simply put, the quality of those decisions determines the quality of our lives.

As believers who have been saved by a loving and merciful God, we have every reason to make wise choices. Yet sometimes, amid the inevitable hustle and bustle of life here on earth, we allow ourselves to behave in ways that we know are displeasing to God. When we do, we forfeit—albeit temporarily—the joy and the peace that we might otherwise experience through Him.

As you consider the next step in your life's journey, take time to consider how many things in this life you can control: your thoughts, your words, your priorities, and your actions, for starters. And then, if you sincerely want to discover God's purpose for your life, make choices that are pleasing to Him. He deserves no less . . . and neither do you.

Let us come near to God with
a sincere heart and a sure faith,
because we have been made free from
a guilty conscience, and our bodies have
been washed with pure water.

—

Hebrews 10:22 NCV

MORE GREAT IDEAS ABOUT CHOICES

There may be no trumpet sound or loud applause when we make a right decision, just a calm sense of resolution and peace.

Gloria Gaither

Every day of our lives we make choices about how we're going to live that day.

Luci Swindoll

God expresses His love in giving us the freedom to choose.

Charles Stanley

No matter how many books you read, no matter how many schools you attend, you're never really wise until you start making wise choices.

Marie T. Freeman

A PRAYER FOR TODAY

Heavenly Father, I have many choices to make. Help me choose wisely as I follow in the footsteps of Your only begotten Son. Amen

The fear of the Lord is the beginning of wisdom, and the knowledge of the Holy One is understanding.

Proverbs 9:10 HCSB

THE RIGHT KIND OF FEAR

D o you have a healthy, fearful respect for God's power? If so, you are both wise and obedient. And, because you are a thoughtful believer, you also understand that genuine wisdom begins with a profound appreciation for God's limitless power.

God praises humility and punishes pride. That's why God's greatest servants will always be those humble men and women who care less for their own glory and more for God's glory. In God's kingdom, the only way to achieve greatness is to shun it. And the only way to be wise is to understand these facts: God is great; He is all-knowing; and He is all-powerful. We must respect Him, and we must humbly obey His commandments, or we must accept the consequences of our misplaced pride.

MORE GREAT IDEAS ABOUT FEARING GOD

A healthy fear of God will do much to deter us from sin.

Charles Swindoll

The remarkable thing about fearing God is that when you fear God, you fear nothing else, whereas if you do not fear God, you fear everything else.

Oswald Chambers

If we do not tremble before God, the world's system seems wonderful to us and pleasantly consumes us.

James Montgomery Boice

It is not possible that mortal men should be thoroughly conscious of the divine presence without being filled with awe.

C. H. Spurgeon

A PRAYER FOR TODAY

Dear Lord, let my greatest fear be the fear of displeasing You. I will strive, Father, to obey Your commandments and seek Your will this day and every day of my life. Amen

Be sober! Be on the alert! Your adversary the Devil is prowling around like a roaring lion, looking for anyone he can devour.

1 Peter 5:8 HCSB

BE ALERT FOR
THE ADVERSARY

Sometimes sin has a way of sneaking up on us. In the beginning, we don't intend to rebel against God—in fact, we don't think much about God at all. We think, instead, about the allure of sin, and we think (quite incorrectly) that sin is "harmless."

If we deny our sins, we allow those sins to flourish. And if we allow sinful behaviors to become habits, we invite certain hardships into our own lives and into the lives of our loved ones.

Sin tears down character. When we yield to the distractions and temptations of this troubled world, we suffer. But God has other intentions, and His plans for our lives do not include sin or denial.

As creatures of free will, we may disobey God whenever we choose, but when we do so, we put ourselves and our loved ones in peril. Why? Because disobedience invites disaster. We cannot sin against God without consequence. We cannot live outside His will without injury.

We cannot distance ourselves from God without hardening our hearts. We cannot yield to the ever-tempting distractions of our world and, at the same time, enjoy God's peace.

Sometimes, in a futile attempt to justify our behaviors, we make a distinction between "big" sins and "little" ones. To do so is a mistake of "big" proportions. Sins of all shapes and sizes have the power to do us great harm. And in a world where sin is big business, that's certainly a sobering thought.

MORE GREAT IDEAS ABOUT SIN

We cannot out-sin God's ability to forgive us.

Beth Moore

Could it be that the greatest sin is simply not to love the Lord your God with all your heart, mind, soul, and strength?

Anne Graham Lotz

An exalted view of God brings a clear view of sin and a realistic view of self.

Henry Blackaby

MORE FROM GOD'S WORD

For though a righteous man falls seven times, he rises again....

Proverbs 24:16 NIV

So let God work his will in you. Yell a loud no to the Devil and watch him scamper. Say a quiet yes to God and he'll be there in no time. Quit dabbling in sin. Purify your inner life. Quit playing the field.

James 4:7-8 MSG

Test all things; hold fast what is good. Abstain from every form of evil.

1 Thessalonians 5:21-22 NKJV

For all have sinned and fall short of the glory of God.

Romans 3:23 NKJV

A PRAYER FOR TODAY

Dear Lord, I am an imperfect human being. When I have sinned, let me repent from my wrongdoings, and let me seek forgiveness—first from You, then from others, and finally from myself. Amen

Rejoice always, pray without ceasing, in everything give thanks; for this is the will of God in Christ Jesus for you.

1 Thessalonians 5:16-18 NKJV

PRAY OFTEN

I s prayer an integral part of your daily life, or is it a hit-or-miss habit? Do you "pray without ceasing," or is your prayer life an afterthought? Do you regularly pray in the quiet moments of the early morning, or do you bow your head only when others are watching?

As Christians, we are instructed to pray often. But it is important to note that genuine prayer requires much more than bending our knees and closing our eyes. Heartfelt prayer is an attitude of the heart.

If your prayers have become more a matter of habit than a matter of passion, you're robbing yourself of a deeper relationship with God. And how can you rectify this situation? By praying more frequently and more fervently. When you do, God will shower you with His blessings, His grace, and His love.

The quality of your spiritual life will be in direct proportion to the quality of your prayer life: the more you pray, the closer you will feel to God. So today, instead of turning things over in your mind, turn them over to God in prayer. Instead of worrying about your next decision, ask God to lead the way. Don't limit your prayers to the dinner table or the bedside table. Pray constantly about things great and small. God is always listening; it's up to you to do the rest.

MORE GREAT IDEAS ABOUT PRAYER

God says we don't need to be anxious about anything; we just need to pray about everything.

Stormie Omartian

What God gives in answer to our prayers will always be the thing we most urgently need, and it will always be sufficient.

Elisabeth Elliot

It is well said that neglected prayer is the birth-place of all evil.

C. H. Spurgeon

When the Holy Spirit comes to dwell within us, I believe we gain a built-in inclination to take our concerns and needs to the Lord in prayer.

Shirley Dobson

MORE FROM GOD'S WORD

So He Himself often withdrew into the wilderness and prayed.

Luke 5:16 NKJV

Therefore I say unto you, What things soever ye desire, w hen ye pray, believe that ye receive them, and ye shall have them.

Mark 11:24 KJV

Your Father knows the things you have need of before you ask Him.

Matthew 6:8 NKJV

A PRAYER FOR TODAY

Dear Lord, make me a person of constant prayer. Your Holy Word commands me to pray without ceasing; let me take everything to You. When I am discouraged, let me pray. When I grieve, let me take my tears to You, Lord, in prayer. When I am uncertain of my next step, let me turn to You for guidance. And, when I am joyful, let me offer up prayers of thanksgiving. In all things great and small, at all times, I will seek Your wisdom and Your Grace . . . in prayer. Amen

Whoever believes that Jesus is the Christ is born of God, and everyone who loves Him who begot also loves him who is begotten of Him.

1 John 5:1 NKJV

GIVE HIM YOUR HEART

Your decision to allow Christ to reign over your heart is the pivotal decision of your life. It is a decision that you cannot ignore. It is a decision that is yours and yours alone.

God's love for you is deeper and more profound than you can imagine. God's love for you is so great that He sent His only Son to this earth to die for your sins and to offer you the priceless gift of eternal life. Now, you must decide whether or not to accept God's gift. Will you ignore it or embrace it? Will you return it or neglect it? Will you accept Christ's love and build a lifelong relationship with Him, or will you turn away from Him and take a different path?

Accept God's gift now: allow His Son to preside over your heart, your thoughts, and your life, starting this very instant.

MORE GREAT IDEAS ABOUT ACCEPTING CHRIST

It's your heart that Jesus longs for: your will to be made His own with self on the cross forever, and Jesus alone on the throne.

Ruth Bell Graham

The amount of power you experience to live a victorious, triumphant Christian life is directly proportional to the freedom you give the Spirit to be Lord of your life!

Anne Graham Lotz

A man can accept what Christ has done without knowing how it works; indeed, he certainly won't know how it works until he's accepted it.

C. S. Lewis

A PRAYER FOR TODAY

Father, You gave Your Son that I might have life eternal. Thank You for this priceless gift and for the joy I feel in my heart when I give You my thoughts, my prayers, my praise, and my life. Amen

Be anxious for nothing, but in everything by prayer and supplication, with thanksgiving, let your requests be made known to God.

Philippians 4:6 NKJV

BEYOND ANXIETY

We live in a world that often breeds anxiety and fear. When we come face to face with tough times, we may fall prey to discouragement, doubt, or depression. But our Father in Heaven has other plans. God has promised that we may lead lives of abundance, not anxiety. In fact, His Word instructs us to "be anxious for nothing." But how can we put our fears to rest? By taking those fears to God and leaving them there.

As you face the challenges of everyday living, do you find yourself becoming anxious, troubled, discouraged, or fearful? If so, turn every one of your concerns over to your Heavenly Father. The same God who created the universe will comfort you if you ask Him . . . so ask Him and trust Him. And then watch in amazement as your anxieties melt into the warmth of His loving hands.

MORE GREAT IDEAS ABOUT ANXIETY

Worry and anxiety are sand in the machinery of life; faith is the oil.

E. Stanley Jones

So often we pray and then fret anxiously, waiting for God to hurry up and do something. All the while God is waiting for us to calm down, so He can do something through us.

Corrie ten Boom

We must lay our questions, frustrations, anxieties, and impotence at the feet of God and wait for His answer. And then receiving it, we must live by faith.

Kay Arthur

A PRAYER FOR TODAY

Forgive me, Lord, when I worry. Worry reflects a lack of trust in Your ability to meet my every need. Help me to work, Lord, and not to worry. And, keep me mindful, Father, that nothing, absolutely nothing, will happen this day that You and I cannot handle together. Amen

Draw near to God, and He will draw near to you.

James 4:8 HCSB

DRAW NEAR TO GOD

I f God is everywhere, why does He sometimes seem so far away? The answer to that question, of course, has nothing to do with God and everything to do with us.

When we begin each day on our knees, in praise and worship to Him, God often seems very near indeed. But, if we ignore God's presence or—worse yet—rebel against it altogether, the world in which we live becomes a spiritual wasteland.

Are you tired, discouraged, or fearful? Be comforted because God is with you. Are you confused? Listen to the quiet voice of your Heavenly Father. Are you bitter? Talk with God and seek His guidance. Are you celebrating a great victory? Thank God and praise Him. He is the Giver of all things good.

In whatever condition you find yourself, wherever you are, whether you are happy or sad, victorious or vanquished, troubled or triumphant, celebrate God's presence. And be comforted. God is not just near; He has promised that He is right here, right now. And that's a promise you can depend on.

MORE GREAT IDEAS ABOUT GOD'S PRESENCE

If you want to hear God's voice clearly and you are uncertain, then remain in His presence until He changes that uncertainty. Often, much can happen during this waiting for the Lord. Sometimes, he changes pride into humility, doubt into faith and peace.

Corrie ten Boom

A sense of deity is inscribed on every heart.

John Calvin

Make the least of all that goes and the most of all that comes. Don't regret what is past. Cherish what you have. Look forward to all that is to come. And most important of all, rely moment by moment on Jesus Christ.

Gigi Graham Tchividjian

A PRAYER FOR TODAY

Heavenly Father, You are with me in times of celebration and in times of sorrow; when I am strong and when I am weak. You never leave my side even when it seems to me that You are far away. Today and every day, God, let me feel You and acknowledge Your presence so that others, too, might know You through me. Amen

The Lord bless you and keep you; the Lord make His face shine upon you, and be gracious to you.

Numbers 6:24-25 NKJV

COUNTING YOUR BLESSINGS

If you sat down and began counting your blessings, how long would it take? A very, very long time! Your blessings include life, freedom, family, friends, talents, and possessions, for starters. But, your greatest blessing—a gift that is yours for the asking—is God's gift of salvation through Christ Jesus.

Today, begin making a list of your blessings. You most certainly will not be able to make a complete list, but take a few moments and jot down as many blessings as you can. Then give thanks to the giver of all good things: God. His love for you is eternal, as are His gifts. And it's never too soon—or too late—to offer Him thanks.

MORE GREAT IDEAS ABOUT BLESSINGS

When you and I are related to Jesus Christ, our strength and wisdom and peace and joy and love and hope may run out, but His life rushes in to keep us filled to the brim. We are showered with blessings, not because of anything we have or have not done, but simply because of Him.

Anne Graham Lotz

Think of the blessings we so easily take for granted: Life itself; preservation from danger; every bit of health we enjoy; every hour of liberty; the ability to see, to hear, to speak, to think, and to imagine all this comes from the hand of God.

Billy Graham

God is more anxious to bestow His blessings on us than we are to receive them.

St. Augustine

A PRAYER FOR TODAY

Lord, I have more blessings than I can possibly count; make me mindful of Your precious gifts. You have cared for me, Lord, and You have saved me. I will give thanks and praise You always. Today, let me share Your blessings with others, just as You first shared them with me. Amen

I the Lord do not change.

Malachi 3:6 HCSB

WHAT DOESN'T CHANGE

We live in a world that is always changing, but we worship the God who never changes—thank goodness! That means that we can be comforted in the knowledge that our Heavenly Father is the rock that simply cannot be moved.

The next time you face difficult circumstances, tough times, unfair treatment, or unwelcome changes, remember that some things never change—things like the love that you feel in your heart for your family and friends . . . and the love that God feels for you. So, instead of worrying too much about life's inevitable challenges, focus your energies on finding solutions. Have faith in your own abilities, do your best to solve your problems, and leave the rest up to God.

MORE GREAT IDEAS ABOUT CHANGE

God has a course mapped out for your life, and all the inadequacies in the world will not change His mind. He will be with you every step of the way. And though it may take time, He has a celebration planned for when you cross over the "Red Seas" of your life.

Charles Swindoll

Both a good marriage and a bad marriage have moments of struggle, but in a healthy relationship, the husband and wife search for answers and areas of agreement because they love each other.

James Dobson

The main joy of heaven will be the heavenly Father greeting us in a time and place of rejoicing, celebration, joy, and great reunion.

Bill Bright

A PRAYER FOR TODAY

Dear Lord, our world changes, but You are unchanging. When I face challenges that leave me discouraged or fearful, I will turn to You for strength and assurance. Let my trust in You—like Your love for me—be unchanging and everlasting. Amen

The man of integrity walks securely, but he who takes crooked paths will be found out.

Proverbs 10:9 NIV

CHARACTER COUNTS

It has been said that character is what we are when nobody is watching. How true. If we sincerely wish to walk with God, we must strive, to the best of our abilities, to follow God's path and to obey His instructions. In short, we must recognize the importance that integrity should play in our lives.

When we listen carefully to the conscience that God has placed within our hearts, and when we behave in ways that are consistent with our beliefs, we can't help but to receive God's blessings.

So today and every day, give yourself a gift by listening carefully to your conscience. Build your life on the firm foundation of integrity. When you do, you won't need to look over your shoulder to see who, besides God, is watching.

MORE GREAT IDEAS ABOUT CHARACTER

In matters of style, swim with the current. In matters of principle, stand like a rock.

Thomas Jefferson

The trials of life can be God's tools for engraving His image on our character.

Warren Wiersbe

There is no way to grow a saint overnight. Character, like the oak tree, does not spring up like a mushroom.

Vance Havner

Character is both developed and revealed by tests, and all of life is a test.

Rick Warren

A PRAYER FOR TODAY

Lord, You are my Father in Heaven. You search my heart and know me far better than I know myself. May I be Your worthy servant, and may I live according to Your commandments. Let me be a person of integrity, Lord, and let my words and deeds be a testimony to You, today and always. Amen

A merry heart does good, like medicine.

Proverbs 17:22 NKJV

CHEERFULNESS IS A GIFT

Cheerfulness is a gift that we give to others and to ourselves. And, as believers who have been saved by a risen Christ, why shouldn't we be cheerful? The answer, of course, is that we have every reason to honor our Savior with joy in our hearts, smiles on our faces, and words of celebration on our lips.

Few things in life are more sad, or, for that matter, more absurd, than grumpy Christians. Christ promises us lives of abundance and joy if we accept His love and His grace. Yet sometimes, even the most righteous among us are beset by fits of ill temper and frustration. During these moments, we may not feel like turning our thoughts and prayers to Christ, but if we seek to gain perspective and peace, that's precisely what we must do.

Are you a cheerful Christian? You should be! And what is the best way to attain the joy that is rightfully yours? By giving Christ what is rightfully His: your heart, your soul, and your life.

MORE GREAT IDEAS ABOUT CHEERFULNESS

Sour godliness is the devil's religion.

John Wesley

The people whom I have seen succeed best in life have always been cheerful and hopeful people who went about their business with a smile on their faces.

Charles Kingsley

Be assured, my dear friend, that it is no joy to God in seeing you with a dreary countenance.

C. H. Spurgeon

We may run, walk, stumble, drive, or fly, but let us never lose sight of the reason for the journey, or miss a chance to see a rainbow on the way.

Gloria Gaither

A PRAYER FOR TODAY

Dear Lord, You have given me so many reasons to celebrate. Today, let me choose an attitude of cheerfulness. Let me be a joyful Christian, Lord, quick to smile and slow to anger. And, let me share Your goodness with all whom I meet so that Your love might shine in me and through me. Amen

Give thanks to the Lord, for He is good; His faithful love endures forever.

Psalm 106:1 HCSB

HIS LOVE ENDURES

God's love for you is bigger and better than you can imagine. In fact, God's love is far too big to comprehend (in this lifetime). But this much we know: God loves you so much that He sent His Son Jesus to come to this earth and to die for you. And, when you accepted Jesus into your heart, God gave you a gift that is more precious than gold: the gift of eternal life. Now, precisely because you are a wondrous creation treasured by God, a question presents itself: What will you do in response to God's love? Will you ignore it or embrace it? Will you return it or neglect it? The decision, of course, is yours and yours alone.

When you embrace God's love, you are forever changed. When you embrace God's love, you feel differently about yourself, your neighbors, and your world. When you embrace God's love, you share His message and you obey His commandments.

When you accept the Father's gift of grace, you are blessed here on earth and throughout all eternity. So do yourself a favor right now: accept God's love with open arms and welcome His Son Jesus into your heart. When you do, your life will be changed today, tomorrow, and forever.

*For the Lord is good,
and His love is eternal;
His faithfulness endures through
all generations.*

—

Psalm 100:5 HCSB

MORE GREAT IDEAS ABOUT GOD'S LOVE

There is no pit so deep that God's love is not deeper still.

Corrie ten Boom

Being loved by Him whose opinion matters most gives us the security to risk loving, too—even loving ourselves.

Gloria Gaither

I love Him because He first loved me, and He still does love me, and He will love me forever and ever.

Bill Bright

Even when we cannot see the why and wherefore of God's dealings, we know that there is love in and behind them, so we can rejoice always.

J. I. Packer

A PRAYER FOR TODAY

Dear Lord, Your Word teaches us that You are love. I will love You, Father, and I will share Your love my family and friends, today and forever. Amen

The LORD is gracious and full of compassion, slow to anger and great in mercy. The LORD is good to all, and His tender mercies are over all His works.

Psalm 145:8-9 NKJV

GOD'S MERCY

I n Psalm 145, we are taught that God is merciful. His hand offers forgiveness and salvation. God's mercy, like His love, is infinite and everlasting—it knows no boundaries.

Romans 3:23 reminds us of a universal truth: "All have sinned, and come short of the glory of God" (KJV). All of us, even the most righteous among us, are sinners. But despite our imperfections, our merciful Father in heaven offers us salvation through the person of His Son.

As Christians, we have been blessed by a merciful, loving God. Now, it's our turn to share His love and His mercy with a world that needs both. May we accept His gifts and share them with our friends, with our families, and with all the people He chooses to place along our paths.

MORE GREAT IDEAS ABOUT GOD'S MERCY

Is your child learning of the love of God through your love, tenderness, and mercy?

James Dobson

Mercy is an attribute of God, an infinite and inexhaustible energy within the divine nature which disposes God to be actively compassionate.

A. W. Tozer

How happy we are when we realize that He is responsible, that He goes before, that goodness and mercy shall follow us!

Mrs. Charles E. Cowman

A PRAYER FOR TODAY

Dear Lord, I have fallen short of Your commandments, and You have forgiven me. You have blessed me with Your love and Your mercy. Enable me to be merciful toward others, Father, just as You have been merciful to me, and let me share Your love with all whom I meet. Amen

Therefore, whatever you want others to do for you, do also the same for them—this is the Law and the Prophets.

Matthew 7:12 HCSB

THE GOLDEN RULE

The words of Matthew 7:12 remind us that, as believers in Christ, we are commanded to treat others as we wish to be treated. This commandment is, indeed, the Golden Rule for Christians of every generation. When we weave the thread of kindness into the very fabric of our lives, we give glory to the One who gave His life for ours.

Because we are imperfect human beings, we are, on occasion, selfish, thoughtless, or cruel. But God commands us to behave otherwise. He teaches us to rise above our own imperfections and to treat others with unselfishness and love. When we observe God's Golden Rule, we help build His kingdom here on earth. And, when we share the love of Christ, we share a priceless gift; may we share it today and every day that we live.

MORE GREAT IDEAS ABOUT THE GOLDEN RULE

The Golden Rule starts at home, but it should never stop there.

Marie T. Freeman

It is one of the most beautiful compensations of life that no one can sincerely try to help another without helping herself.

Barbara Johnson

Your light is the truth of the Gospel message itself as well as your witness as to Who Jesus is and what He has done for you. Don't hide it.

Anne Graham Lotz

A PRAYER FOR TODAY

Dear Lord, let me treat others as I wish to be treated. Because I expect kindness, let me be kind. Because I wish to be loved, let me be loving. Because I need forgiveness, let me be merciful. In all things, Lord, let me live by the Golden Rule, and let me teach that rule to others through my words and my deeds. Amen

Cast thy burden upon the LORD, and he shall sustain thee: he shall never suffer the righteous to be moved.

Psalm 55:22 KJV

WHERE TO PLACE YOUR BURDENS

God's Word contains promises upon which we, as Christians, can and must depend. The Bible is a priceless gift, a tool that God intends for us to use in every aspect of our lives. Too many Christians, however, keep their spiritual tool kits tightly closed and out of sight.

Psalm 55:22 instructs us to cast our burdens upon the Lord. And that's perfect advice for men, women, and children alike.

Are you tired? Discouraged? Fearful? Be comforted and trust the promises that God has made to you. Are you worried or anxious? Be confident in God's power. He will never desert you. Do you see a difficult future ahead? Be courageous and call upon God. He will protect you and then use you according to His purposes. Are you confused? Listen to the quiet voice of your Heavenly Father. He is not a God of confusion. Talk with Him; listen to Him; trust Him, and trust His promises.

MORE GREAT IDEAS ABOUT GOD'S SUPPORT

Measure the size of the obstacles against the size of God.

Beth Moore

God uses our most stumbling, faltering faith-steps as the open door to His doing for us "more than we ask or think."

Catherine Marshall

The last and greatest lesson that the soul has to learn is the fact that God, and God alone, is enough for all its needs. This is the lesson that all His dealings with us are meant to teach; and this is the crowning discovery of our whole Christian life. God is enough!

Hannah Whitall Smith

A PRAYER FOR TODAY

Heavenly Father, You never leave or forsake me. You are always with me, protecting me and encouraging me. Whatever this day may bring, I thank You for Your love and Your strength. Let me lean upon You, Father, this day and forever. Amen

No temptation has overtaken you except such as is common to man; but God is faithful, who will not allow you to be tempted beyond what you are able, but with the temptation will also make the way of escape, that you may be able to bear it.

1 Corinthians 10:13 NKJV

RESISTING TEMPTATION

It's inevitable: today you will be tempted by somebody or something—in fact, you will probably be tempted many times. Why? Because you live in a world that is filled to the brim with temptations! Some of these temptations are small; eating a second scoop of ice cream, for example, is enticing but not very dangerous. Other temptations, however, are not nearly so harmless.

The devil is working 24/7, and he's causing pain and heartache in more ways than ever before. We, as believers, must remain watchful and strong. And the good news is this: When it comes to fighting Satan, we are never alone. God is always with us, and He gives us the power to resist temptation whenever we ask Him to give us strength.

In a letter to believers, Peter offered a stern warning: "Your adversary, the devil, prowls around like a roaring lion, seeking someone to devour" (1 Peter 5:8 NASB). As Christians, we must take that warning seriously, and we must behave accordingly.

MORE GREAT IDEAS ABOUT TEMPTATION

Lord, what joy to know that Your powers are so much greater than those of the enemy.

Corrie ten Boom

There is sharp necessity for giving Christ absolute obedience. The devil bids for our complete self-will. To whatever extent we give this self-will the right to be master over our lives, we are, to an extent, giving Satan a toehold.

Catherine Marshall

Instant intimacy is one of the leading warning signals of a seduction.

Beth Moore

It is easier to stay out of temptation than to get out of it.

Rick Warren

Deception is the enemy's ongoing plan of attack.

Stormie Omartian

MORE FROM GOD'S WORD

My son, if sinners entice you, do not consent.

Proverbs 1:10 NKJV

Listen for God's voice in everything you do, everywhere you go; he's the one who will keep you on track. Don't assume that you know it all. Run to God! Run from evil!

Proverbs 3:6-7 MSG

Jesus responded, "I assure you: Everyone who commits sin is a slave of sin."

John 8:34 HCSB

And lead us not into temptation; but deliver us from evil.

Luke 11:4 KJV

A PRAYER FOR TODAY

Dear Lord, this world is filled with temptations, distractions, and frustrations. When I turn my thoughts away from You and Your Word, Lord, I suffer bitter consequences. But, when I trust in Your commandments, I am safe. Direct my path far from the temptations and distractions of the world. Let me discover Your will and follow it, Dear Lord, this day and always. Amen

So he who had received five talents came and brought five other talents, saying, "Lord, you delivered to me five talents; look, I have gained five more talents besides them." His lord said to him, "Well done, good and faithful servant; you were faithful over a few things, I will make you ruler over many things. Enter into the joy of your lord."

Matthew 25:20-21 NKJV

USING YOUR TALENTS

The old saying is both familiar and true: "What we are is God's gift to us; what we become is our gift to God." Each of us possesses special talents, gifted by God, that can be nurtured carefully or ignored totally. Our challenge, of course, is to use our abilities to the greatest extent possible and to use them in ways that honor our Savior.

Are you using your natural talents to make God's world a better place? If so, congratulations. But if you have gifts that you have not fully explored and developed, perhaps you need to have a chat with the One who gave you those gifts in the first place. Your talents are priceless treasures offered from your Heavenly Father. Use them. After all, an obvious way to say "thank you" to the Giver is to use the gifts He has given.

MORE GREAT IDEAS ABOUT TALENTS

In the great orchestra we call life, you have an instrument and a song, and you owe it to God to play them both sublimely.

Max Lucado

You are a unique blend of talents, skills, and gifts, which makes you an indispensable member of the body of Christ.

Charles Stanley

Employ whatever God has entrusted you with, in doing good, all possible good, in every possible kind and degree.

John Wesley

A PRAYER FOR TODAY

Father, You have given me abilities to be used for the glory of Your kingdom. Give me the courage and the perseverance to use those talents. Keep me mindful that all my gifts come from You, Lord. Let me be Your faithful, humble servant, and let me give You all the glory and all the praise. Amen

Be strong and courageous, and do the work. Don't be afraid or discouraged, for the Lord God, my God, is with you. He won't leave you or forsake you.

1 Chronicles 28:20 HCSB

COURAGE FOR TODAY

C hristians have every reason to live courageously. After all, the ultimate battle has already been won on the cross at Calvary. But even dedicated followers of Christ may find their courage tested by the inevitable disappointments and fears that visit the lives of believers and non-believers alike.

When you find yourself worried about the challenges of today or the uncertainties of tomorrow, you must ask yourself whether or not you are ready to place your concerns and your life in God's all-powerful, all-knowing, all-loving hands. If the answer to that question is yes—as it should be—then you can draw courage today from the source of strength that never fails: your Heavenly Father.

MORE GREAT IDEAS ABOUT COURAGE

Courage is contagious.

Billy Graham

The truth of Christ brings assurance and so removes the former problem of fear and uncertainty.

A. W. Tozer

If a person fears God, he or she has no reason to fear anything else. On the other hand, if a person does not fear God, then fear becomes a way of life.

Beth Moore

Our Lord is searching for people who will make a difference. Christians dare not dissolve into the background or blend into the neutral scenery of the world.

Charles Swindoll

A PRAYER FOR TODAY

Dear Lord, fill me with Your Spirit and help me face my challenges with courage and determination. Keep me mindful, Father, that You are with me always—and with You by my side, I have nothing to fear. Amen

Don't be deceived: God is not mocked. For whatever a man sows he will also reap, because the one who sows to his flesh will reap corruption from the flesh, but the one who sows to the Spirit will reap eternal life from the Spirit.

Galatians 6:7-8 HCSB

CHOOSE WISELY

L ife is a series of choices. Each day, we make countless decisions that can bring us closer to God… or not. When we live according to God's commandments, we earn for ourselves the abundance and peace that He intends for our lives. But, when we turn our backs upon God by disobeying Him, we bring needless suffering upon ourselves and our families.

Do you seek God's peace and His blessings? Then obey Him. When you're faced with a difficult choice or a powerful temptation, seek God's counsel and trust the counsel He gives. Invite God into your heart and live according to His commandments. When you do, you will be blessed today, and tomorrow, and forever.

MORE GREAT IDEAS ABOUT BEHAVIOR

Our response to God determines His response to us.

Henry Blackaby

Don't worry about what you do not understand. Worry about what you do understand in the Bible but do not live by.

Corrie ten Boom

More depends on my walk than my talk.

D. L. Moody

There may be no trumpet sound or loud applause when we make a right decision, just a calm sense of resolution and peace.

Gloria Gaither

A PRAYER FOR TODAY

Dear Lord, let my words and actions show the world the changes that You have made in my life. You sent Your Son so that I might have abundant life and eternal life. Thank You, Father, for my Savior, Christ Jesus. I will follow Him, honor Him, and share His Good News, this day and every day. Amen

"Follow Me," Jesus told them, "and I will make you into fishers of men!" Immediately they left their nets and followed Him.

Mark 1:17-18 HCSB

DISCIPLESHIP NOW

When Jesus addressed His disciples, He warned that each one must "take up his cross and follow Me." The disciples must have known exactly what the Master meant. In Jesus' day, prisoners were forced to carry their own crosses to the location where they would be put to death. Thus, Christ's message was clear: in order to follow Him, Christ's disciples must deny themselves and, instead, trust Him completely. Nothing has changed since then.

If we are to be disciples of Christ, we must trust Him and place Him at the very center of our beings. Jesus never comes "next." He is always first. The paradox, of course, is that only by sacrificing ourselves to Him do we gain salvation for ourselves.

Do you seek to be a worthy disciple of Christ? Then pick up His cross today and every day that you live. When you do, He will bless you now and forever.

MORE GREAT IDEAS ABOUT DISCIPLESHIP

Jesus challenges you and me to keep our focus daily on the cross of His will if we want to be His disciples.

Anne Graham Lotz

When Jesus put the little child in the midst of His disciples, He did not tell the little child to become like His disciples; He told the disciples to become like the little child.

Ruth Bell Graham

Our devotion to God is strengthened when we offer Him a fresh commitment each day.

Elizabeth George

A PRAYER FOR TODAY

Help me, Lord, to understand what cross I am to bear this day. Give me the strength and the courage to carry that cross along the path of Your choosing so that I may be a worthy disciple of Your Son. Amen

Immediately the father of the child cried out and said with tears, "Lord, I believe; help my unbelief!"

Mark 9:24 NKJV

BEYOND THE DOUBTS

E ven the most faithful Christians are overcome by occasional bouts of fear and doubt. You are no different. When you feel that your faith is being tested to its limits, seek the comfort and assurance of the One who sent His Son as a sacrifice for you.

Have you ever felt your faith in God slipping away? If so, you are not alone. Every life—including yours—is a series of successes and failures, celebrations and disappointments, joys and sorrows, hopes and doubts.

But even when you feel very distant from God, remember that God is never distant from you. When you sincerely seek His presence, He will touch your heart, calm your fears, and restore your soul.

MORE GREAT IDEAS ABOUT DOUBTS

Seldom do you enjoy the luxury of making decisions that are based on enough evidence to absolutely silence all skepticism.

Bill Hybels

A life lived in God is not lived on the plane of feelings, but of the will.

Elisabeth Elliot

Fear and doubt are conquered by a faith that rejoices. And faith can rejoice because the promises of God are as certain as God Himself.

Kay Arthur

A PRAYER FOR TODAY

Dear God, sometimes this world can be a puzzling place, filled with uncertainty and doubt. When I am unsure of my next step, keep me mindful that You are always near and that You can overcome any challenge. Give me faith, Father, and let me remember always that with Your love and Your power, I can live courageously and faithfully today and every day. Amen

Now may the God of hope fill you with all joy and peace in believing, so that you may overflow with hope by the power of the Holy Spirit.

Romans 15:13 HCSB

BIG DREAMS

Are you willing to entertain the possibility that God has big plans in store for you? Hopefully so. Yet sometimes, especially if you've recently experienced a life-altering disappointment, you may find it difficult to envision a brighter future for yourself and your family. If so, it's time to reconsider your own capabilities . . . and God's.

Your Heavenly Father created you with unique gifts and untapped talents; your job is to tap them. When you do, you'll begin to feel an increasing sense of confidence in yourself and in your future.

It takes courage to dream big dreams. You will discover that courage when you do three things: accept the past, trust God to handle the future, and make the most of the time He has given you today.

Nothing is too difficult for God, and no dreams are too big for Him—not even yours. So start living—and dreaming—accordingly.

MORE GREAT IDEAS ABOUT DREAMS

The future lies all before us. Shall it only be a slight advance upon what we usually do? Ought it not to be a bound, a leap forward to altitudes of endeavor and success undreamed of before?

Annie Armstrong

You cannot out-dream God.

John Eldredge

To make your dream come true, you have to stay awake.

Dennis Swanberg

Set goals so big that unless God helps you, you will be a miserable failure.

Bill Bright

A PRAYER FOR TODAY

Dear Lord, give me the courage to dream and the faithfulness to trust in Your perfect plan. When I am worried or weary, give me strength for today and hope for tomorrow. Keep me mindful of Your healing power, Your infinite love, and Your eternal salvation. Amen

For I know the thoughts that I think toward you, says the Lord, thoughts of peace and not of evil, to give you a future and a hope. Then you will call upon Me and go and pray to Me, and I will listen to you.

Jeremiah 29:11-12 NKJV

YOUR VERY BRIGHT FUTURE

B ecause we are saved by a risen Christ, we can have hope for the future, no matter how troublesome our present circumstances may seem. After all, God has promised that we are His throughout eternity. And, He has told us that we must place our hopes in Him.

Of course, we will face disappointments and failures while we are here on earth, but these are only temporary defeats. This world can be a place of trials and tribulations, but when we place our trust in the Giver of all things good, we are secure. God has promised us peace, joy, and eternal life. And God keeps His promises today, tomorrow, and forever.

Are you willing to place your future in the hands of a loving and all-knowing God? Do you trust in the ultimate goodness of His plan for your life? Will you face today's challenges with optimism and hope? You should. After all, God created you for a very important purpose: His purpose. And you still have important work to do: His work.

Today, as you live in the present and look to the future, remember that God has a plan for you. Act—and believe—accordingly.

My cup runs over. Surely goodness and mercy shall follow me all the days of my life; and I will dwell in the house of the Lord forever.

—

Psalm 23:5-6 NKJV

MORE GREAT IDEAS ABOUT THE FUTURE

You can look forward with hope, because one day there will be no more separation, no more scars, and no more suffering in My Father's House. It's the home of your dreams!

Anne Graham Lotz

Every experience God gives us, every person he brings into our lives, is the perfect preparation for the future that only he can see.

Corrie ten Boom

Allow your dreams a place in your prayers and plans. God-given dreams can help you move into the future He is preparing for you.

Barbara Johnson

A PRAYER FOR TODAY

Dear Lord, as I look to the future, I will place my trust in You. If I become discouraged, I will turn to You. If I am afraid, I will seek strength in You. You are my Father, and I will place my hope, my trust, and my faith in You. Amen

Whoever serves me must follow me. Then my servant will be with me everywhere I am. My Father will honor anyone who serves me.

John 12:26 NCV

FOLLOWING HIS FOOTSTEPS

Each day, we make countless decisions that can bring us closer to God . . . or not. When we live according to God's commandments, we reap bountiful rewards: abundance, hope, and peace, for starters. But, when we turn our backs upon God by disobeying Him, we bring needless suffering upon ourselves and our families.

Do you seek to walk in the footsteps of the One from Galilee, or will you choose another path? If you sincerely seek God's peace and His blessings, then you must strive to imitate God's Son.

Thomas Brooks spoke for believers of every generation when he observed, "Christ is the sun, and all the watches of our lives should be set by the dial of his motion." Christ, indeed, is the ultimate Savior of mankind and the personal Savior of those who believe in Him. As His servants, we should walk in His footsteps as we share His love and His message with a world that needs both.

MORE GREAT IDEAS ABOUT IMITATING CHRIST

Every Christian is to become a little Christ. The whole purpose of becoming a Christian is simply nothing else.

C. S. Lewis

Prayer makes a godly man and puts within him "the mind of Christ," the mind of humility, of self-surrender, of service, and of piety. If we really pray, we will become more like God, or else we will quit praying.

E. M. Bounds

The steady discipline of intimate friendship with Jesus results in men becoming like Him.

Harry Emerson Fosdick

A PRAYER FOR TODAY

Dear Lord, You sent Your Son so that I might have abundant life and eternal life. Thank You, Father, for my Savior, Christ Jesus. I will follow Him, honor Him, and share His Good News, this day and every day. Amen

My cup runs over. Surely goodness and mercy shall follow me all the days of my life; and I will dwell in the house of the Lord Forever.

Psalm 23:5-6 NKJV

OPTIMISTIC CHRISTIANITY

Pessimism and Christianity don't mix. Why? Because Christians have every reason to be optimistic about life here on earth and life eternal. As C. H. Spurgeon observed, "Our hope in Christ for the future is the mainstream of our joy." But sometimes, we fall prey to worry, frustration, anxiety, or sheer exhaustion, and our hearts become heavy. What's needed is plenty of rest, a large dose of perspective, and God's healing touch, but not necessarily in that order.

Today, make this promise to yourself and keep it: vow to be a hope-filled Christian. Think optimistically about your life, your profession, your future, and your family. Trust your hopes, not your fears. Take time to celebrate God's glorious creation. And then, when you've filled your heart with hope and gladness, share your optimism with others. They'll be better for it, and so will you. But not necessarily in that order.

MORE GREAT IDEAS ABOUT OPTIMISM

The popular idea of faith is of a certain obstinate optimism: the hope, tenaciously held in the face of trouble, that the universe is fundamentally friendly and things may get better.

J. I. Packer

It is a remarkable thing that some of the most optimistic and enthusiastic people you will meet are those who have been through intense suffering.

Warren Wiersbe

The Christian lifestyle is not one of legalistic do's and don'ts, but one that is positive, attractive, and joyful.

Vonette Bright

A PRAYER FOR TODAY

Lord, let me be an expectant Christian. Let me expect the best from You, and let me look for the best in others. If I become discouraged, Father, turn my thoughts and my prayers to You. Let me trust You, Lord, to direct my life. And, let me be Your faithful, hopeful, optimistic servant every day that I live. Amen

Rejoice in hope; be patient in affliction; be persistent in prayer.

Romans 12:12 HCSB

THE POWER OF PATIENCE

Most of us are impatient for God to grant us the desires of our heart. Usually, we know what we want, and we know precisely when we want it: right now, if not sooner. But God may have other plans. And when God's plans differ from our own, we must trust in His infinite wisdom and in His infinite love.

As busy men and women living in a fast-paced world, many of us find that waiting quietly for God is difficult. Why? Because we are fallible human beings seeking to live according to our own timetables, not God's. In our better moments, we realize that patience is not only a virtue, but it is also a commandment from God.

God instructs us to be patient in all things. We must be patient with our families, our friends, and our associates. We must also be patient with our Heavenly Father as He unfolds His plan for our lives. And that's as it should be. After all, think about how patient God has been with us.

MORE GREAT IDEAS ABOUT PATIENCE

If God is diligent, surely we ought to be diligent in doing our duty to Him. Think how patient and diligent God has been to us!

Oswald Chambers

Waiting is the hardest kind of work, but God knows best, and we may joyfully leave all in His hands.

Lottie Moon

The next time you're disappointed, don't panic. Don't give up. Just be patient and let God remind you he's still in control.

Max Lucado

A PRAYER FOR TODAY

Dear Lord, You have been so patient with me, and I praise You for Your forgiveness. Make me Your patient servant. When I am hurried, slow me down. When I become angry, give me empathy. Make me a patient Christian, Father, as I trust in You and in Your master plan. Amen

And the peace of God, which surpasses every thought, will guard your hearts and your minds in Christ Jesus. Finally brothers, whatever is true, whatever is honorable, whatever is just, whatever is pure, whatever is lovely, whatever is commendable—if there is any moral excellence and if there is any praise—dwell on these things.

Philippians 4:7-8 HCSB

GENUINE PEACE

Sometimes, peace can be a scarce commodity in a demanding, 21st-century world. How, then, can we find the peace that we so desperately desire? By turning our days and our lives over to God.

The Scottish preacher George McDonald observed, "It has been well said that no man ever sank under the burden of the day. It is when tomorrow's burden is added to the burden of today that the weight is more than a man can bear. Never load yourselves so, my friends. If you find yourselves so loaded, at least remember this: it is your own doing, not God's. He begs you to leave the future to Him."

May we give our lives, our hopes, our prayers, and our futures to the Father, and, by doing so, accept His will and His peace.

MORE GREAT IDEAS ABOUT PEACE

We're prone to want God to change our circumstances, but He wants to change our character. We think that peace comes from the outside in, but it comes from the inside out.

Warren Wiersbe

God's peace is like a river, not a pond. In other words, a sense of health and well-being, both of which are expressions of the Hebrew *shalom,* can permeate our homes even when we're in white-water rapids.

Beth Moore

What peace can they have who are not at peace with God?

Matthew Henry

A PRAYER FOR TODAY

Dear Lord, the peace that the world offers is fleeting, but You offer a peace that is perfect and eternal. Let me take my concerns and burdens to You, Father, and let me feel the spiritual abundance that You offer through the person of Your Son, the Prince of Peace. Amen

The one who acquires good sense loves himself; one who safeguards understanding finds success.

Proverbs 19:8 HCSB

PERSPECTIVE FOR TODAY

If a temporary loss of perspective has left you worried, exhausted, or both, it's time to readjust your thought patterns. Negative thoughts are habit-forming; thankfully, so are positive ones. With practice, you can form the habit of focusing on God's priorities and your own possibilities. When you do, you'll soon discover that you will spend less time fretting about your challenges and more time praising God for His gifts.

When you call upon the Lord and prayerfully seek His will, He will give you wisdom and perspective. When you make God's priorities your priorities, He will direct your steps and calm your fears. So today and every day hereafter, pray for a sense of balance and perspective. And remember: no problems are too big for God—and that includes yours.

MORE GREAT IDEAS ABOUT PERSPECTIVE

Live near to God, and so all things will appear to you little in comparison with eternal realities.

Robert Murray McCheyne

Like a shadow declining swiftly . . . away . . . like the dew of the morning gone with the heat of the day; like the wind in the treetops, like a wave of the sea, so are our lives on earth when seen in light of eternity.

Ruth Bell Graham

Earthly fears are no fears at all. Answer the big questions of eternity, and the little questions of life fall into perspective.

Max Lucado

A PRAYER FOR TODAY

Dear Lord, give me wisdom and perspective. Guide me according to Your plans for my life and according to Your commandments. And keep me mindful, Dear Lord, and that Your truth is—and will forever be—the ultimate truth. Amen

For am I now trying to win the favor of people, or God? Or am I striving to please people? If I were still trying to please people, I would not be a slave of Christ.

Galatians 1:10 HCSB

CHOOSING TO PLEASE GOD

Whom will you try to please today: God or man? Your primary obligation is not to please imperfect men and women. Your obligation is to strive diligently to meet the expectations of an all-knowing and perfect God.

Sometimes, because you're an imperfect human being, you may become so wrapped up in meeting society's expectations that you fail to focus on God's expectations. To do so is a mistake of major proportions—don't make it. Instead, seek God's guidance as you focus your energies on becoming the best "you" that you can possibly be. And, when it comes to matters of conscience, seek approval not from your peers, but from your Creator.

MORE GREAT IDEAS ABOUT PLEASING GOD

It is impossible to please God doing things motivated by and produced by the flesh.

Bill Bright

You must never sacrifice your relationship with God for the sake of a relationship with another person.

Charles Stanley

You will get untold flak for prioritizing God's revealed and present will for your life over man's . . . but, boy, is it worth it.

Beth Moore

A PRAYER FOR TODAY

Dear Lord, today I will honor You with my thoughts, my actions, and my prayers. I will seek to please You, and I will strive to serve You. Your blessings are as limitless as Your love. And because I have been so richly blessed, I will worship You, Father, with thanksgiving in my heart and praise on my lips, this day and forever. Amen

But encourage each other daily, while it is still called today, so that none of you is hardened by sin's deception.

Hebrews 3:13 HCSB

THE POWER OF ENCOURAGEMENT

Life is a team sport, and all of us need occasional pats on the back from our teammates. As Christians, we are called upon to spread the Good News of Christ, and we are also called to spread a message of encouragement and hope to the world.

Whether you realize it or not, many people with whom you come in contact every day are in desperate need of a smile or an encouraging word. The world can be a difficult place, and countless friends and family members may be troubled by the challenges of everyday life. Since you don't always know who needs your help, the best strategy is to try to encourage all the people who cross your path. So today, be a world-class source of encouragement to everyone you meet. Never has the need been greater.

MORE GREAT IDEAS ABOUT ENCOURAGEMENT

Make it a rule, and pray to God to help you to keep it, never to lie down at night without being able to say: "I have made at least one human being a little wiser, a little happier, or a little better this day."

Charles Kingsley

No journey is complete that does not lead through some dark valleys. We can properly comfort others only with the comfort we ourselves have been given by God.

Vance Havner

God is still in the process of dispensing gifts, and He uses ordinary individuals like us to develop those gifts in other people.

Howard Hendricks

A PRAYER FOR TODAY

Dear Lord, make a source of genuine, lasting encouragement to my family and friends. And, let my words and deeds be worthy of Your Son, the One who gives me strength and salvation. Today, Father, I will celebrate Your blessings, and I will share Your Good News with those who cross my path. Amen

In all your ways acknowledge Him, and He shall direct your paths.

Proverbs 3:6 NKJV

SEEKING GOD'S GUIDANCE

When we genuinely seek to know the heart of God—when we prayerfully seek His wisdom and His will—our Heavenly Father carefully guides us over the peaks and valleys of life. And as Christians, we can be comforted: Whether we find ourselves at the pinnacle of the mountain or the darkest depths of the valley, the loving heart of God is always there with us.

As Christians whose salvation has been purchased by the blood of Christ, we have every reason to live joyously and courageously. After all, Christ has already fought and won our battle for us—He did so on the cross at Calvary. But despite Christ's sacrifice, and despite God's promises, we may become confused or disoriented by the endless complications and countless distractions of modern life.

If you're unsure of your next step, lean upon God's promises and lift your prayers to Him. Remember that God is always near; remember that He is your protector and your deliverer. Open yourself to His heart, and Trust Him to guide your path. When you do, God will direct your steps, and you will receive His blessings today, tomorrow, and throughout eternity.

MORE GREAT IDEAS ABOUT GOD'S GUIDANCE

Walk in the daylight of God's will because then you will be safe; you will not stumble.

Anne Graham Lotz

If we want to hear God's voice, we must surrender our minds and hearts to Him.

Billy Graham

It is a joy that God never abandons His children. He guides faithfully all who listen to His directions.

Corrie ten Boom

A PRAYER FOR TODAY

Dear Lord, Thank You for You constant presence and Your constant love. I draw near to You this day with the confidence that You are ready to guide me. Help me walk closely with You, Father, and help me share Your Good News with all who cross my path. Amen

But when the Helper comes, whom I shall send to you from the Father, the Spirit of truth who proceeds from the Father, He will testify of Me.

John 15:26 NKJV

FILLED WITH THE HOLY SPIRIT

Are you burdened by the pressures of everyday living? If so, it's time to ease the pressure. How can you do it? By allowing the Holy Spirit to fill you and to do His work in your life.

When you are filled with the Holy Spirit, your words and deeds will reflect a love and devotion to God. When you are filled with the Holy Spirit, the steps of your life's journey are guided by the Creator of the universe. When you allow God's Spirit to work in you and through you, you will be energized and transformed.

So today, take God at His word. He has promised to fill you with His Spirit if you let Him. Let Him. And then stand back in amazement as the Father begins to work miracles in your own life and in the lives of those you love.

MORE GREAT IDEAS ABOUT THE HOLY SPIRIT

The church needs the power and the gifts of the Holy Spirit more now than ever before.

Corrie ten Boom

The Holy Spirit will not come to us in his fullness until we see and assent to his priority—his passion for ministry.

Catherine Marshall

We have given too much attention to methods and to machinery and to resources, and too little to the Source of Power, the filling with the Holy Ghost.

J. Hudson Taylor

God wants to teach us that when we commit our lives to Him, He gives us that wonderful teacher, the Holy Spirit.

Gloria Gaither

A PRAYER FOR TODAY

Dear Lord, You are my sovereign God. Your Son defeated death; Your Holy Spirit comforts and guides me. Let me celebrate all Your gifts, Father, and let me be a hope-filled Christian today and every day. Amen

On the first day of the week, very early in the morning, they came to the tomb, bringing the spices they had prepared. They found the stone rolled away from the tomb. They went in but did not find the body of the Lord Jesus. While they were perplexed about this, suddenly two men stood by them in dazzling clothes. So the women were terrified and bowed down to the ground. "Why are you looking for the living among the dead?" asked the men. "He is not here, but He has been resurrected!"

Luke 24:1-6 HCSB

CONSIDERING THE RESURRECTION

When we consider the resurrection of Christ, we marvel at God's power, His love, and His mercy. And if God is for us, what can we possibly have to fear? The answer, of course, is that those who have been saved by our living Savior have absolutely nothing to fear.

As we consider the meaning of Christ's life, His death, and His resurrection, we are reminded that God's most precious gift, His only Son, went to Calvary as a sacrifice for a sinful world. May we, as believers who have been saved by the blood of Christ, trust the promises of our Savior. And may we honor Him with our words, our deeds, our thoughts, and our prayers—not only today but also throughout all eternity.

MORE GREAT IDEAS ABOUT THE RESURRECTION

The world has never been stable. Jesus Himself was born into the cruelest and most unstable of worlds. No, we have babies and keep trusting and living because the Resurrection is true! The Resurrection was not just a one-time event in history; it is a principle built into the very fabric of our beings, a fact reverberating from every cell of creation: Life wins! Life wins!

Gloria Gaither

The Resurrection was a proclamation that Christ had conquered sin, death, and the devil. It guarantees there is life beyond the grave.

Charles Stanley

The Resurrection is the biggest news in history. CNN ought to put it on Headline News every thirty minutes. It should scream from every headline: Jesus is alive!

Dennis Swanberg

MORE FROM GOD'S WORD

What a God we have! And how fortunate we are to have him, this Father of our Master Jesus! Because Jesus was raised from the dead, we've been given a brand-new life and have everything to live for, including a future in heaven—and the future starts now!

1 Peter 1:3-4 MSG

For I know that my Redeemer lives.

Job 19:25 NKJV

Though He was delivered up according to God's determined plan and foreknowledge, you used lawless people to nail Him to a cross and kill Him. God raised Him up, ending the pains of death, because it was not possible for Him to be held by it.

Acts 2:23-24 HCSB

A PRAYER FOR TODAY

Dear Jesus, You are my Savior and my protector. You suffered on the cross for me, and I will give You honor and praise every day of my life. I will honor You with my words, my thoughts, and my prayers. And I will live according to Your commandments, so that thorough me, others might come to know Your perfect love. Amen

Now we want each of you to demonstrate the same diligence for the final realization of your hope, so that you won't become lazy, but imitators of those who inherit the promises through faith and perseverance.

Hebrews 6:11-12 HCSB

ENERGY FOR TODAY

All of us have moments when we feel exhausted. All of us suffer through tough times, difficult days, and perplexing periods of our lives. Thankfully, God promises to give us comfort and strength if we turn to Him.

If you're a person with too many demands and too few hours in which to meet them, it's probably time to examine your priorities while you pare down your daily to-do list. While you're at it, take time to focus upon God and His love for you. Then, ask Him for the wisdom to prioritize your life and the strength to fulfill your responsibilities. God will give you the energy to do the most important things on today's to-do list if you ask Him. So ask Him . . . today.

MORE GREAT IDEAS ABOUT ENERGY

Worry does not empty tomorrow of its sorrow; it empties today of its strength.

Corrie ten Boom

God does not dispense strength and encouragement like a druggist fills your prescription. The Lord doesn't promise to give us something to take so we can handle our weary moments. He promises us Himself. That is all. And that is enough.

Charles Swindoll

When we reach the end of our strength, wisdom, and personal resources, we enter into the beginning of his glorious provisions.

Patsy Clairmont

A PRAYER FOR TODAY

Lord, let me find my strength in You. When I am weary, give me rest. When I feel overwhelmed, let me look to You for my priorities. Let Your power be my power, Lord, and let Your way be my way, today and forever. Amen

The one who conceals his sins will not prosper, but whoever confesses and renounces them will find mercy.

Proverbs 28:13 HCSB

MAKING A MISTAKE

E verybody makes mistakes, and so will you. In fact, Winston Churchill once observed, "Success is going from failure to failure without loss of enthusiasm." What was good for Churchill is also good for you. You should expect to make mistakes—plenty of mistakes—but you should not allow those missteps to rob you of the enthusiasm you need to fulfill God's plan for your life.

We are imperfect people living in an imperfect world; mistakes are simply part of the price we pay for being here. But, even though mistakes are an inevitable part of life's journey, repeated mistakes should not be. When we commit the inevitable blunders of life, we must correct them, learn from them, and pray for the wisdom not to repeat them. When we do, our mistakes become lessons, and our lives become adventures in growth, not stagnation.

Have you made a mistake or three? Of course you have. But here's the big question: have you used your mistakes as stumbling blocks or stepping stones? The answer to that question will determine how well you will perform in every aspect of your life.

MORE GREAT IDEAS ABOUT MISTAKES

Sin is largely a matter of mistaken priorities. Any sin in us that is cherished, hidden, and not confessed will cut the nerve center of our faith.

Catherine Marshall

Mistakes offer the possibility for redemption and a new start in God's kingdom. No matter what you're guilty of, God can restore your innocence.

Barbara Johnson

A PRAYER FOR TODAY

Lord, thank You for Your forgiveness and for Your unconditional love. Show me the error of my ways, Lord, that I might confess my wrongdoing and correct my mistakes. And, let me grow each day in wisdom, in faith, and in my love for You. Amen

Let us lay aside every weight and the sin that so easily ensnares us, and run with endurance the race that lies before us, keeping our eyes on Jesus, the source and perfecter of our faith.

Hebrews 12:1-2 HCSB

WHAT'S YOUR FOCUS?

What is your focus today? Are you willing to focus your thoughts and energies on God's blessings and upon His will for your life? Or will you turn your thoughts to other things? Before you answer that question, consider this: God created you in His own image, and He wants you to experience joy and abundance. But, God will not force His joy upon you; you must claim it for yourself.

This day—and every day hereafter—is a chance to celebrate the life that God has given you. It's also a chance to give thanks to the One who has offered you more blessings than you can possibly count.

Today, why not focus your thoughts on the joy that is rightfully yours in Christ? Why not take time to celebrate God's glorious creation? When you do, you will think optimistically about yourself and your world and you can then share your optimism with others. They'll be better for it, and so will you.

MORE GREAT IDEAS ABOUT FOCUS

What is your focus today? Joy comes when it is Jesus first, others second . . . then you.

Kay Arthur

Measure the size of the obstacles against the size of God.

Beth Moore

We need to stop focusing on our lacks and stop giving out excuses and start looking at and listening to Jesus.

Anne Graham Lotz

When Jesus is in our midst, He brings His limitless power along as well. But, Jesus must be in the middle, all eyes and hearts focused on Him.

Shirley Dobson

A PRAYER FOR TODAY

Dear Lord, help me to face this day with a spirit of optimism and thanksgiving. And let me focus my thoughts on You and Your incomparable gifts. Amen

Now finally, all of you should be like-minded and sympathetic, should love believers, and be compassionate and humble.

1 Peter 3:8 HCSB

BUILDING FELLOWSHIP

Your association with fellow Christians should be uplifting, enlightening, encouraging, and consistent. In short, fellowship with other believers should be an integral part of your everyday life.

Are you an active member of your own fellowship? Are you a builder of bridges inside the four walls of your church and outside it? Do you contribute to God's glory by sharing your time and your talents with a close-knit band of believers? Hopefully so. The fellowship of believers is intended to be a powerful tool for spreading God's Good News and uplifting His children. And God intends for you to be a fully contributing member of that fellowship. Your intentions should be the same.

MORE GREAT IDEAS ABOUT FELLOWSHIP

It is wonderful to have all kinds of human support systems, but we must always stand firm in God and in Him alone.

Joyce Meyer

Be united with other Christians. A wall with loose bricks is not good. The bricks must be cemented together.

Corrie ten Boom

I hope you will find a few folks who walk with God to also walk with you through the seasons of your life.

John Eldredge

If you dine alone, you miss the best part of the meal: the fellowship.

Dennis Swanberg

A PRAYER FOR TODAY

Heavenly Father, You have given me a community of supporters called the church. Let our fellowship be a reflection of the love we feel for each other and the love we feel for You. Amen

The one who is from God listens to God's words. This is why you don't listen, because you are not from God.

John 8:47 HCSB

LISTENING TO GOD

Sometimes God speaks loudly and clearly. More often, He speaks in a quiet voice—and if you are wise, you will be listening carefully when He does. To do so, you must carve out quiet moments each day to study His Word and sense His direction.

Can you quiet yourself long enough to listen to your conscience? Are you attuned to the subtle guidance of your intuition? Are you willing to pray sincerely and then to wait quietly for God's response? Hopefully so. Usually God refrains from sending His messages on stone tablets or city billboards. More often, He communicates in subtler ways. If you sincerely desire to hear His voice, you must listen carefully, and you must do so in the silent corners of your quiet, willing heart.

MORE GREAT IDEAS ABOUT LISTENING TO GOD

We cannot experience the fullness of Christ if we do all the expressing. We must allow God to express His love, will, and truth to us.

Gary Smalley

When we come to Jesus stripped of pretensions, with a needy spirit, ready to listen, He meets us at the point of need.

Catherine Marshall

In prayer, the ear is of first importance. It is of equal importance with the tongue, but the ear must be named first. We must listen to God.

S. D. Gordon

A PRAYER FOR TODAY

Dear Lord, I have so much to learn and You have so much to teach me. Give me the wisdom to be still and the discernment to hear Your voice, today and every day. Amen

Six days shall work be done, but the seventh day is a Sabbath of solemn rest, a holy convocation. You shall do no work on it; it is the Sabbath of the Lord in all your dwellings.

Leviticus 23:3 NKJV

KEEPING THE SABBATH

When God gave Moses the Ten Commandments, it became perfectly clear that our Heavenly Father intends for us to make the Sabbath a holy day, a day for worship, for contemplation, for fellowship, and for rest. Yet, we live in a seven-day-a-week world, a world that all too often treats Sunday as a regular workday.

One way to strengthen your character is by giving God at least one day each week. If you carve out the time for a day of worship and praise, you'll be amazed at the impact it will have on the rest of your week. But if you fail to honor God's day, if you treat the Sabbath as a day to work or a day to party, you'll miss out on a harvest of blessings that is only available one day each week.

How does your family observe the Lord's day? When church is over, do you treat Sunday like any other day of the week? If so, it's time to think long and hard about your family's schedule and your family's priorities. And if

223

you've been treating Sunday as just another day, it's time to break that habit. When Sunday rolls around, don't try to fill every spare moment. Take time to rest . . . Father's orders!

MORE GREAT IDEAS ABOUT THE SABBATH

It is what Jesus is, not what we are, that gives rest to the soul. If we really want to overcome Satan and have peace with God, we must "fix our eyes on Jesus." Let his death, his suffering, his glories, and his intercession be fresh on your mind.

C. H. Spurgeon

Jesus gives us the ultimate rest, the confidence we need, to escape the frustration and chaos of the world around us.

Billy Graham

One reason so much American Christianity is a mile wide and an inch deep is that Christians are simply tired. Sometimes you need to kick back and rest for Jesus' sake.

Dennis Swanberg

MORE FROM GOD'S WORD

For the Son of Man is the Lord of the Sabbath.

Matthew 12:8 NIV

What's important in all this is that if you keep a holy day, keep it for God's sake; if you eat meat, eat it to the glory of God and thank God for prime rib; if you're a vegetarian, eat vegetables to the glory of God and thank God for broccoli.

Romans 14:6 MSG

Worship the Lord with gladness. Come before him, singing with joy. Acknowledge that the Lord is God! He made us, and we are his. We are his people, the sheep of his pasture.

Psalm 100:2-3 NLT

Then He told them, "The Sabbath was made for man, and not man for the Sabbath.

Mark 2:27 HCSB

A PRAYER FOR TODAY

Dear Lord, I thank You for the Sabbath day, a day when I can worship You and praise Your Son. I will keep the Sabbath as a holy day, a day when I can honor You. Amen

Cast your burden on the Lord, and He shall sustain you; He shall never permit the righteous to be moved.

Psalm 55:22 NKJV

OVERCOMING STRESS

Stressful days are an inevitable fact of modern life. And how do we best cope with the challenges of our demanding world? By turning our days and our lives over to God. Elisabeth Elliot writes, "If my life is surrendered to God, all is well. Let me not grab it back, as though it were in peril in His hand but would be safer in mine!" Yet even the most devout Christian may, at times, seek to grab the reins of their life and proclaim, "I'm in charge!" To do so is foolish, prideful, and stressful.

When we seek to impose our own wills upon the world—or upon other people—we invite stress into our lives . . . needlessly. But, when we turn our lives and our hearts over to God—when we accept His will instead of seeking vainly to impose our own—we discover the inner peace that can be ours through Him.

Do you feel overwhelmed by the stresses of daily life? Turn your concerns and your prayers over to God. Trust Him. Trust Him completely. Trust Him today. Trust Him always. When it comes to the inevitable challenges of this day, hand them over to God completely and without reservation. He knows your needs and will meet those needs in His own way and in His own time if you let Him.

MORE GREAT IDEAS ABOUT STRESS

When frustrations develop into problems that stress you out, the best way to cope is to stop, catch your breath, and do something for yourself, not out of selfishness, but out of wisdom.

Barbara Johnson

The better acquainted you become with God, the less tensions you feel and the more peace you possess.

Charles Allen

The happiest people I know are the ones who have learned how to hold everything loosely and have given the worrisome, stress-filled, fearful details of their lives into God's keeping.

Charles Swindoll

Don't be overwhelmed. Take it one day and one prayer at a time.

Stormie Omartian

MORE FROM GOD'S WORD

Then they cried out to the Lord in their trouble, and He saved them out of their distresses.

Psalm 107:13 NKJV

For You, O God, have tested us; You have refined us as silver is refined. You brought us into the net; You laid affliction on our backs. You have caused men to ride over our heads; we went through fire and through water; but You brought us out to rich fulfillment

Psalm 66:10–12 NKJV

Rejoice in hope; be patient in affliction; be persistent in prayer.

Romans 12:12 HCSB

A PRAYER FOR TODAY

Heavenly Father, You never leave or forsake me. Even when I am troubled by the demands of the day, You are always with me, protecting me and encouraging me. Whatever today may bring, I thank You for Your love and Your strength. Let me lean upon You, Father, this day and forever. Amen

I am the door. If anyone enters by Me, he will be saved, and will come in and go out and find pasture.

John 10:9 HCSB

THE GIFT OF SALVATION

How marvelous it is that God's Son walked among us. Had He not chosen to do so, we might feel removed from a distant Creator. But ours is not a distant God. Ours is a God who understands—far better than we ever could—the essence of what it means to be human.

God understands our hopes, our fears, and our temptations. He understands what it means to be angry and what it costs to forgive. He knows the heart, the conscience, and the soul of every person who has ever lived, including you. And God has a plan of salvation that is intended for you. Accept it. Accept God's gift through the person of His Son Christ Jesus, and then rest assured: God walked among us so that you might have eternal life; amazing though it may seem, He did it for you.

MORE GREAT IDEAS ABOUT SALVATION

Our salvation comes to us so easily because it cost God so much.

Oswald Chambers

Personal salvation is not an occasional rendezvous with Deity; it is an actual dwelling with God.

Billy Graham

God's goal is not to make you happy. It is to make you his.

Max Lucado

Today is the day of salvation. Some people miss heaven by only eighteen inches—the distance between their heads and their hearts.

Corrie ten Boom

A PRAYER FOR TODAY

Dear Lord, You sent Your Son as the Savior of our world. Jesus is my Savior, Lord, and my strength. I will share His Good News with all who cross my path, and I will share His love with all who need His healing touch. Amen

Thanks be to God for His indescribable gift.

2 Corinthians 9:15 HCSB

A THANKFUL HEART

Sometimes, life can be complicated, demanding, and frustrating. When the demands of life leave us rushing from place to place with scarcely a moment to spare, we may fail to pause and thank our Creator for the countless blessings He bestows upon us. But, whenever we neglect to give proper thanks to the Giver of all things good, we suffer because of our misplaced priorities.

As believers who have been saved by a risen Christ, we are blessed beyond human comprehension. We who have been given so much should make thanksgiving a habit, a regular part of our daily routines. Of course, God's gifts are too numerous to count, but we should attempt to count them nonetheless. We owe our Heavenly Father everything, including our eternal praise . . . starting right now.

MORE GREAT IDEAS ABOUT
THANKSGIVING

The words "thank" and "think" come from the same root word. If we would think more, we would thank more.

Warren Wiersbe

God often keeps us on the path by guiding us through the counsel of friends and trusted spiritual advisors.

Bill Hybels

If you won't fill your heart with gratitude, the devil will fill it with something else.

Marie T. Freeman

The act of thanksgiving is a demonstration of the fact that you are going to trust and believe God.

Kay Arthur

A PRAYER FOR TODAY

Dear Lord, sometimes, amid the demands of the day, I lose perspective, and I fail to give thanks for Your blessings and for Your love. Today, help me to count those blessings, and let me give thanks to You, Father, for Your love, for Your grace, for Your blessings, and for Your Son. Amen

After this manner therefore pray ye: Our Father which art in heaven, Hallowed be thy name. Thy kingdom come. Thy will be done in earth, as it is in heaven. Give us this day our daily bread. And forgive us our debts, as we forgive our debtors. And lead us not into temptation, but deliver us from evil: For thine is the kingdom, and the power, and the glory, for ever. Amen

Matthew 6:9-13 KJV

THE LORD'S PRAYER

"Our Father which art in heaven, hallowed be thy name." These familiar words begin the Lord's Prayer, a prayer that you've heard on countless occasions. It's the prayer that Jesus taught His followers to pray, and it's a prayer that you probably know by heart.

You already know what the prayer says, but have you thought carefully, and in detail, about exactly what those words mean? Hopefully so. After all, this simple prayer was authored by the Savior of mankind.

Today, take the time to carefully consider each word in this beautiful passage. When you weave the Lord's Prayer into the fabric of your life, you'll soon discover that God's Word and God's Son have the power to change everything, including you.

MORE GREAT IDEAS ABOUT GOD

God is the beyond in the midst of our life.

Dietrich Bonhoeffer

God has put into each of our lives a void that cannot be filled by the world. We may leave God or put Him on hold, but He is always there, patiently waiting for us . . . to turn back to Him.

Emilie Barnes

God is not a supernatural interferer; God is the everlasting portion of his people. When a man born from above begins his new life, he meets God at every turn, hears him in every sound, sleeps at his feet, and wakes to find him there.

Oswald Chambers

A PRAYER FOR TODAY

Dear Lord, when I pray, let me feel Your presence. When I worship You, let me feel Your love. In the quiet moments of the day, I will open my heart to You, Almighty God. And I know that You are with me always and that You will always hear my prayers. Amen

I was glad when they said unto me, let us go into the house of the LORD.

Psalm 122:1 KJV

OUR NEED TO WORSHIP GOD

All of humanity is engaged in worship. The question is not whether we worship, but what we worship. Wise men and women choose to worship God. When they do, they are blessed with a plentiful harvest of joy, peace, and abundance. Other people choose to distance themselves from God by foolishly worshiping things that are intended to bring personal gratification but not spiritual gratification. Such choices often have tragic consequences.

If we place our love for material possessions above our love for God—or if we yield to the countless temptations of this world—we find ourselves engaged in a struggle between good and evil, a clash between God and Satan. Our responses to these struggles have implications that echo throughout our families and throughout our communities.

How can we ensure that we cast our lot with God? We do so, in part, by the practice of regular, purposeful worship in the company of fellow believers. When we worship God faithfully and fervently, we are blessed. When we fail to worship God, for whatever reason, we forfeit the spiritual gifts that He intends for us.

We must worship our Heavenly Father, not just with our words, but also with our deeds. We must honor Him, praise Him, and obey Him. As we seek to find purpose and meaning for our lives, we must first seek His purpose and His will. For believers, God comes first. Always first.

Do you place a high value on the practice of worship? Hopefully so. After all, every day provides countless opportunities to put God where He belongs: at the very center of your life. It's up to you to worship God seven days a week; anything less is simply not enough.

Worship the Lord your God and . . .
serve Him only.

—

Matthew 4:10 HCSB

MORE GREAT IDEAS ABOUT WORSHIP

In the sanctuary, we discover beauty: the beauty of His presence.

Kay Arthur

God has promised to give you all of eternity. The least you can do is give Him one day a week in return.

Marie T. Freeman

I am of the opinion that we should not be concerned about working for God until we have learned the meaning and delight of worshipping Him.

A. W. Tozer

A PRAYER FOR TODAY

When I worship You, Lord, You direct my path and You cleanse my heart. Let today and every day be a time of worship and praise. Let me worship You in everything that I think and do. Thank You, Lord, for the priceless gift of Your Son Jesus. Let me be worthy of that gift, and let me give You the praise and the glory forever. Amen

Go, therefore, and make disciples of all nations, baptizing them in the name of the Father and of the Son and of the Holy Spirit, teaching them to observe everything I have commanded you. And remember, I am with you always, to the end of the age.

Matthew 28:19-20 HCSB

THE GREAT COMMISSION

A re you a bashful Christian, one who is afraid to speak up for your Savior? Do you leave it up to others to share their testimonies while you stand on the sidelines, reluctant to share yours? Too many of us are slow to obey the last commandment of the risen Christ; we don't do our best to "make disciples of all the nations."

Christ's Great Commission applies to Christians of every generation, including our own. As believers, we are commanded to share the Good News with our families, with our neighbors, and with the world. Jesus invited His disciples to become fishers of men. We, too, must accept the Savior's invitation, and we must do so today. Tomorrow may indeed be too late.

MORE GREAT IDEAS ABOUT THE GREAT COMMISSION

There are many timid souls whom we jostle morning and evening as we pass them by; but if only the kind word were spoken they might become fully persuaded.

Fanny Crosby

There is nothing anybody else can do that can stop God from using us. We can turn everything into a testimony.

Corrie ten Boom

Your light is the truth of the Gospel message itself as well as your witness as to Who Jesus is and what He has done for you. Don't hide it.

Anne Graham Lotz

A PRAYER FOR TODAY

Dear Lord, let me share the Good News of Your Son Jesus. Let the life that I live and the words that I speak be a witness to my faith in Him. And let me share the story of my salvation with others so that they, too, might receive His eternal gifts. Amen

*Be of good courage,
and He shall strengthen your heart,
all you who hope in the Lord.*

—

Psalm 31:24 NKJV